LOCKED JAWS

"Partake as doth the bee
Abstemiously—"

—Emily Dickinson

"Everything I like is either immoral,
illegal, or fattening."

—G. B. Shaw

"I am large. I contain multitudes."

—Walt Whitman

"One is what he eats."

—Goethe

"I have always maintained that the popular notion of connecting excessive grossness of size and excessive good-humour as inseparable allies was equivalent to declaring, either that no people but amiable people ever get fat, or that the accidental addition of so many pounds of flesh has a directly favourable influence over the disposition of the person on whose body they accumulate."

—Wilkie Collins, in
The Woman in White,
of Count Fosco

"Lord, you have taught me to use food as a medicine."

—St. Augustine, *Confessions*

"A goodly portly man, i'faith, and a corpulent."

—Falstaff, of himself,
Henry IV, Part I

"Banish plump Jack, and banish all the world."

—Falstaff, again of
himself

"If I do grow great, I'll grow less."

—Falstaff

"Study, therefore, to withdraw the love of your soul from all things that are visible, and to turn it to things that are invisible. Those who follow their own sensuality hurt their own cause . . ."

—Thomas a Kempis,
The Imitation of Christ

"Instead of three meals a day, if it be necessary eat but one; instead of a hundred dishes, five."

—H. D. Thoreau

". . . for temptations of gluttony, inasmuch as they arise from natural bodily senses, are the hardest sins to avoid."

—Walter Hilton,
The Ladder of Perfection

"We are determined to be starved before we are hungry."

—H. D. Thoreau

"Everything you put in *shows!*"

—Aunt Minnie

Books by Nick Lyons

Jones Very: Selected Poems (ed.)

The Seasonable Angler

Fisherman's Bounty (ed.)

Fishing Widows

The Sony Vision

Bright Rivers

Locked Jaws

LOCKED JAWS

The Tragical-
Historical-
Comical

JOURNAL
OF A DIETER

in Quest of a
Youthful Figure

NICK LYONS

Illustrated by
J-C Suarès

Crown Publishers, Inc.
New York

Printed in the United States of America
Published simultaneously in Canada by General Publishing Company Limited

Sections of this book originally appeared, in somewhat different form, in *The Pennsylvania Gazette*. © 1977, 1978 by *The Pennsylvania Gazette*. Used by permission.

Library of Congress Cataloging in Publication Data

Lyons, Nick.
    Locked Jaws.

1. Reducing diets—Anecdotes, facetiae, satire, etc.
I. Title.
RM222.2.L97 1979   613.2'5'0207   79-14937
ISBN 0-517-53855-5

Jacket and book design by J-C Suarès

I am neither a doctor nor a health expert. This is merely a personal record, essentially true, though some names have been changed and I have garnished the facts a little here and there. I must insist you read it at your own risk.

CONTENTS

2061592

For BEATRICE BLUMENAU who always has the best advice

PREFACE

I began this melancholy journal for a specific and selfish purpose. Unlike the man who joins the circus so he can write first hand about circuses, I started to write so I would be forced by the pen to diet. The diet was long overdue: I had become a blimp.

The weight had come on slowly, over a strenuous period in my life lasting some twenty years. Like many middle-aged Americans, I was exercising too little, worrying too much, and blithely eating myself into oblivion. Most things I do I do with zeal, and I had become a zealous glutton.

I weigh 165 now—and may, I hope, weigh somewhat less by the time my manuscript reaches print—a loss of more than fifty pounds. And that is another purely selfish reason for having written this book: print carries finality, and I want to force myself to *stay* thin. Committing myself to print and then undoing what all this monstrous struggle has wrought would be an ultimate humiliation.

Beyond my selfish reasons—and I am no advocate of altruism—perhaps an account of my sad struggles will benefit others who, in their middle years, find themselves in an alien body. I hope so. Anyway, I am positive that *anyone* willing to undergo severe food-deprivation for the rest of his life can also lose fifty pounds. There is no trick to it at all: no gimmick, no miracle. A lot of tongue-in-cheek helps. But more than anything else, it merely takes *a firm lock on your jaws*.

—Nick Lyons

ONE

Desperate Struggles

It may have begun when the bed collapsed. My wife merely pouted but my four wiseacre children began to sing, with ten imaginative stanzas to it,

"O, Nicholas, O, Nicholas,
Your belly is ri-dic-u-lous."

It was. And I began, soon afterward, the preliminary and important step of *thinking* about dieting. I thought about it for five months, growing fatter by the day, angrier at myself with every pound.

Yesterday was the turning point. Clearly it was the man at Hamburger Heaven. He could not have weighed less than 350 pounds, perhaps more. His stomach protruded over the table-top like yeast expanding out of a heated pot; he looked at the food on his plate for nearly five minutes with the most extraordinary relish—and then he went to work.
What a sight to behold!

He stuffed a Behemoth Burger into his behemoth maw, chawed with abandon, picked particles of tomato and hamburger off his napkin and nicely placed them into the furnace, too. Then he licked his fingers and began on a second one. He could barely move. He out-ate Oblomov. Two cokes, then a third. Four bags of french fried potatoes. Three hot apple turnovers. A strawberry malted. Another hot apple turnover. Then he started to eat more slowly. Was he finally filled, sated? Hardly. By his look, he merely wanted the food to last longer. He dreaded to eat the last morsel.

At last, finished with every possible scrap on his tray, having swiped even the top of a hamburger roll someone had abandoned at the next table and licked clean the turnover cardboards, he breathed deeply and held his cup of soda to the light, to see if there was any Coke left, hiding below the ice.

There was none.

He shook his head philosophically, smiled wanly, and licked a finger.

I had been watching the scene motionless, astonished, stunned. When the man finished—when he had finished absolutely and ate merely with his eyes—I began my own meal. I rammed the Behemoth Burger into my mouth and kept watching him, mesmerized. On my third bite, he took one last wistful look at his tray, sighed contentedly, and began to squoosh his way out—O, so slowly—from behind the table. As he did so—his eyes leaving his tray for the first moment since I had seen him—he saw me, the hamburger stuffed into my mouth, my jaws working furiously.

It was his smile that finally convinced me.

He looked at me eating and with a sigh of recognition knew I was his brother of the plate—a younger brother, not quite so experienced, but on the way up. And I recognized that this was what he

thought—and that this might well be so. We were both out of George Grosz by way of upper Broadway. We were addicts, food machines, gluttons. It took one to know one.

I would not let it be so. It was a mistake, a charade. I was not such a person. Somewhere inside me, crouched and ready to leap out again, was the slim basketball player I had been in college, seventy pounds earlier.

My mid-forties—and already 220 pounds. It was a terrible mistake. I threw down the rest of the hamburger and rushed out. I would reform. I would stop eating. Altogether. I would play basketball again, regain the past. I had seen and now I knew and I would *will* it otherwise. Had I been unconscious all those years?

Didn't I nearly collapse when I ran twenty feet for a bus? Wasn't there a message in that?

Weren't the missing shirt buttons a clue?

Hadn't I been warned when my fishing waders would not go over my thighs?

Shouldn't I have suspected something when, at business lunches, I broke the seams in the crotch of my pants and had to hobble, legs close, behind someone to the coat rack?

Today I have started this diet. God help me, I will not stop until I am a skinny man.

Tomorrow I'll start to exercise.

SECOND DAY

Too weak to write.

THIRD DAY

Do I really think I can survive for the rest of my life without a decent meal? Fat chance. It's unthinkable.

I fasted until three o'clock the first day, then grew dizzy, even faint, and finally rushed into the kitchen. A moment's hesitation, then—*poof, poof*—three slices of bread were gone before one could say "strawberry shortcake." Yesterday I had two boiled eggs for breakfast, a tossed salad for lunch, and chopped meat (broiled) for supper. My head was so light I felt I'd lost it.

And today? Don't ask.

This was a year-long day. I thought food all morning at the publishing office, then raced uptown during my lunch break to work on a ghostwriting assignment. For two hours I became the woman; I vanished; I felt my voice change and my hormones wiggle. Then, after three crunching hours back at work, I raced up to school and delivered a two-hour diatribe on Falstaff, that great horseback-breaker, lover of greasy capon and sack. Banish plump Jack, banish his love of food—mountains of food, of sweet, sour, spiced, fatty, caloric foods—and surely you banish all the world. Everybody laughed. Surely I am my own best visual aid for a lecture like this. I loved it. They loved it. I got so caught up in my talk that, to illustrate Hal's statement that you'd need a derrick to raise a fallen Falstaff, I lay down on the floor—and could not get up.

But then one mean-spirited literalist raised his hand and said: "Excuse me, Professor Lyons, but didn't you assign *Poe* for today?"

On my way home I ate half a hot pretzel before I knew I had bought the thing.

This is hell. I cannot possibly survive another day of such brutal pain.

And why should I? There are thousands of fat men who are perfectly fit and happy. The country is prejudiced against fat—that's the fat truth of it. Look at the slim shapes in every ad. Only thin people have fun. Only thin people can be elegant, successful. Mari is prejudiced against it, too, and has begun to reinforce her prejudice with a certain reserve.

And my four children are perfect bigots!

My belly is "ri-di-cu-lous," eh? Not only do I have every good reason to be fat—overwork, financial worries, anxiety about the very wiseacre children who mock me—but I *like* being fat, I like to eat, and I find absolutely nothing immoral, illegal, or unaesthetic about it.

I have read that fat men make better lovers; I

know two superb fat poets; I know fat octogenar-
ians; Chesterton was a mountain of a man; Balzac
was short, but not a mouse; Rembrandt was no
peanut.

Are there religious, moral, medical proscriptions
against fat? Does it really affect your health? Bigotry.
Narrow-minded bigotry is all. And vanity.

Anyway, I have a large frame.

The fact is, my body does not *want* to lose weight.
The scale, after all this starvation, shows the loss,
perhaps, if I stand lightly on it—reaching for sky
hooks—of one measely pound. Also, I have constipation.

Tomorrow is destined to be a new beginning. My
new motto is: *Food without guilt!*

Fried eggs, four slices of toast, and sausage for

breakfast again. Pizza, spaghetti, veal parmigiana, franks and beans. Cherry cheesecake and rainbow cookies and seven-layer cake and strawberry tarts! Old friends. Great, reliable sources of energy and good cheer. Dear allies. Beer. Salami and Ritz crackers at midnight. Chocolate cherries, on the run, after breakfast. Smoked salmon and pâté and pressed apricot sheets and sugar jellies from Zabar's.

Yes!

FOURTH DAY

Pure gluttony, pure delight.

FIFTH DAY

I survived my temporary insanity—will avoid the sad details—and am on course again. Salads are supposed to be good for this business so I am eating greens at every meal.

I have resolved, definitely, to begin a rigorous exercise program. In a few days. Maybe a week.

The severe pains and dizziness of the first days have almost disappeared. Will my stomach, in time, grow used to less food? So it seems—tonight.

There appears to be some connection between this eating and the rest of my affairs. That third day was typical of the smorgasbord, my life. I am too busy. I am too often someone else. I do too much that I do not want to be doing. Everything and everyone irritates me. I do not like the Big Apple. I do not like even the words "Big Apple." I want to be in Montana. Or Chile. Or Alaska. I want to wade wild rivers, fish for trout and truth, not live this noisy desperation.

Merely thinking about my busyness and what and where I'd like to be makes me hungry.

Mari's reserve is no help.

Maybe exercise will help. I'll do some tomorrow. Or the next day.

SIXTH DAY

I managed to get through this one—but only barely. I kept thinking of all the money I owe the Internal Revenue Service, my silent partner. I have

written them four long letters, explaining in great
detail that I made so much money last year because
I worked three jobs, or was it four, or five, full time
each, and used the money to pay old debts and
Dracula, my bank. I have received no reply. Un-
communicative fellows. Still, thinking about them
out there wanting their money, with their hungry
computers working overtime, I lost three games of
chess to my boys—crunching games that nearly
drove me, with all my other worries, to eat. But I
resisted and am proud of myself.

I even tried some push-ups but could not yet do
one. Once I could do fifty. Mari told me to get up
off the floor and stop groaning and acting like a
stuck pig. I told her to mind her goddam business.

The scale tells me I have lost three pounds already.

An auspicious start!

SEVENTH DAY　　　　　　　　　*Soliloquy upon a Strudel*

O, that this too too solid flesh would melt,
Thaw, and resolve itself into a sylph,
Or that the Everlasting had not fixt my flesh
With such a lousy metabolism. O, God!
How weary, stale, flat, and unprofitable
Seem to me all the uses of fried foods!
They are an unweedable garden
That make me rank and gross in nature.
That it should come to this! Two hundred and
　　　seventeen pounds—
Must I remember? Why, I would hang on tarts
As if increase of appetite could grow
By what it fed on; and yet, within a week,
I am brought to near starvation.
Let me not think on't. Frailty, thy name was Nick!

Thou didst bestride the caloric world
Like a colossus—feed thy great maw with wicked
    speed,
Bear the thousand natural shocks that flesh is heir
    to,
And turn pale thought to a cheesecake orgy.
O, my offense is rank; it smells of capon;
It hath the sin of gluttony upon it
And will with surety remove me from this mortal
    coil
Lest I take arms against this culinary riot
And by starvation, end it.
            To fast, to starve—
Perchance to die of it! Ah, there's the rub.

(He takes strudel in his hand and holds it above eye
level; violins in background)

Alas, poor strudel, I knew thee well—
A fellow of infinite jest, of excellent fancy—
Yet now how abhorred in my imagination.
    Again the hungry lion roars.
My gorge rises at it: I must merely look.
A week since and you'd have come to lips—
    Again the hungry lion roars—
But break my eye, for I must hold my tongue.

EIGHTH DAY

There is a photograph of me taken when I was twenty-one. I am rising up off the court for a lay-up; the basketball is poised high in my right hand, my cheeks are pinched, my thighs are slim, my eye is fixed on the rim of the basket, and my size 29 pants are—amazingly—beginning to slip down from my waist. Mari dug it out last night, left it on my desk without comment, and it has haunted me since. I took it to the mirror and compared that fiery dynamo, that flash of thin steel, with the frumpy, flabby, jowled figure I saw in the glass. Impossible. I was never that thin.

The picture has stuck in my brain all day—the lithe figure frozen in midair, the tooled tautness of the calves, the sharply pinched cheeks.

Is it possible to be that person again? Could I really ever slip from this fleshy sheath I have taken on and find that Attic form again? Could I touch the rim, run with the kids, regain some fraction of that old, hard-won grace?

That person seems very far away; I cannot even climb into that boy's head, let alone regain his body.

I tried to think of the boy's dreams and hopes—to

do a few good things wisely and well. And I thought of the scurry and carelessness and small cheatings, and the trading of one's skills for a handful of gold dust that, anyway, in due course, would only fall to the IRS.

Only a lot of starvation and some hard exercise will bring back something of those days, those dreams. I must attack the problem as a total, all-out war—not limited, prudent, strategic warfare. I must increase the number of push-ups to two, at least, by tomorrow. My dietary goal should be, *No food whatsoever*. Zilch. That is perfection.

I have read about a woman who advocates fasting. She claims that it helps her spiritually to eliminate the ''morbid fat.'' She also advocates regular enemas to eliminate the ''morbid matter.'' This zealous woman speaks of the great benefits to skin, lungs, kidneys, bowels, liver, brought about by fasting. The nervous system is rejuvenated, mental powers improved.

She does not mention if the IRS gives you credit for all this.

But fasting is quite impossible for me. The nagging ache in my stomach never subsides. Maybe I'm not normal, but I do not feel spiritually higher when I miss a meal, only dizzy. I still think food almost every minute of the day. The withdrawal symptoms are unbearable. Mari would have me committed if I bought an enema bag.

By tomorrow I should be able to do three push-ups and perhaps half a dozen sit-ups. How I'd love to play basketball again!

And every day, in every way, that thin young dreamer is borne back ceaselessly into the past.

NINTH DAY

The look of my body in the bathtub tonight—festooned with flab, my breasts and thighs monstrous! The frightening displacement of water.

How could I *ever* have let it come to this? My children now regularly call me "Dads."

I thought of the butcher I had watched this afternoon, shaving the thick white fat from a whole filet mignon, in globs.

How I envy some people their metabolism: their beautiful, gorgeous metabolism.

TENTH DAY

A friend who experienced the true light via a consciousness-raising discipline—one of those ten thousand improvement-of-self groups which proliferate like roaches—tells me my eating is a survival tape, that I need food to survive.

"Hell, I know that," I said.

"No. Deeper survival than that. Survival in the most primitive, eco-biomorphic-historioso sense. Clearly you don't need so much food to survive *physically*. But you associate lack of food with 'not-surviving,' surviving negativistically. When you're worried about survival, your tapes go onto automatic and you remember something in your childhood. Go off automatic, man. Find the seed that sparks the tape."

So I sat quietly this evening and went back to my childhood, and got to my fourth year. I was being sent to a boarding school, which I did not like. I was being given for lunch that day my favorite foods, as a kind of last lunch. My favorite foods happened to be cucumbers and chicken, low in calories. And then, thinking back, I got to the desperate loneliness I had felt in that great gray building in Peekskill, and how much I enjoyed my mother bringing me strawberry cream cake—ah, ha!—several week-ends. I remembered the strawberry cream cake and some particular boxes of candy extremely well.

Surely food pacifies and I have always been hyperactive, a bit too worried about whether I would survive, but those memories did not seem strong enough to have caused much mischief. Nor do the days when various relatives forced me to eat broccoli and spinach, which later made me vomit. Now if I had asked for "more," and had to face Mr. Bumble . . .

I remember a friend whose mother would sit him in a high chair, with a bib—when the kid was

thirteen—and stuff him, every morning without fail, with a tasty mixture of oatmeal and black bananas. Like a goose. He was thirty pounds overweight at the time, and she was a string bean. Now, in his early forties, *he* is a string bean and she has ulcers.

My children, who eat amply, are all skinny as railposts. Mari is thin. Do you inherit obesity? Or is it acquired by hard work?

What's all this news about fat cells?

Maybe I have a rotten thyroid.

When I played basketball in college I ate not much less than I do now, though of course I ran around like a rabbit six or eight hours a day.

I could survive quite nicely if it weren't for the IRS. *They* are the true villains.

ELEVENTH DAY

"The jig's up," Mari said after dinner tonight. "I saw what you did. You're a fraud. I tried to believe that you were serious about all this dieting but now I'll never trust you again."

I was astounded. No one could be hungrier than I was.

"You're not getting away with that again," she said. "Unless, of course, you merely want to keep up this charade of dieting, this sham."

"I don't know what you mean."

"I've been watching you carefully. You're becoming a secret eater—and right under my eye. I suspected so. Now I'm positive."

"All I had for dinner was salad. Not a scrap more. I've been eating only salad for days. I'm starved. You saw what I ate."

"I saw."

"So?"

"Who made the salad?"

"I did."

"What did you smuggle into it?"

"That salad was mostly lettuce."

"And what else?"

"Lettuce. Lettuce . . . and a few tomatoes. I don't remember anything else."

"You don't remember putting in a handful of olives, a quarter of a pound of sliced cheese, four or five slices of ham, and—God help you—half a salami?"

"It was only a chef's salad."

"Chef's, indeed! And the dressing? Three times as much oil as vinegar. Do you have the slightest idea how many calories are in olive oil? And sugar. Anchovies. Chopped olives. At least a full table-spoon of salt. Salt!"

"Only rabbits eat it raw."

"And how many portions did you take?"

"A few. Do you want me to starve? It was only salad."

"*Seven* portions is not a few and will surely not lead to starvation. And while we're at it, you're only fooling yourself by eating fruit all day. There are *eight* apples missing and the children ate none of them. I asked."

"You're a fiend. A spy. You're worse than the IRS."

Silence.

"Fruit is good for you. Roughage. Bulk. Think of my constipation."

"Eight apples a day is as bad as eight slices of bread or two portions of strawberry shortcake."

"I could survive contentedly on two portions of strawberry shortcake a day. I thought I'd have to go the rest of my life, another forty years, without straw-berry shortcake."

"If you don't stop smuggling down such quantities of food you won't last another four years," she said.

And then she said, quietly, with a seriousness of purpose that quite terrified me: "I read recently about a woman who lost seventy pounds by having her jaws wired shut."

TWELFTH DAY   No doubt to encourage me, Mari mentioned casually today that a friend of a friend had lost 125

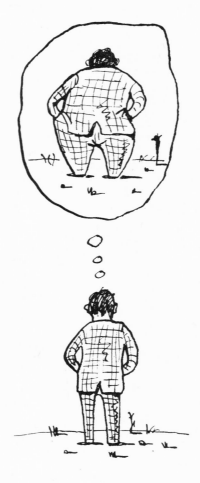

pounds in six months. "Everyone," she said, "said he looked perfectly marvelous. They couldn't believe it."

Instead of being encouraged by this story—perhaps the tenth such story I've heard this week—I could not help thinking how much pleasure the man must have had putting *on* the 125 pounds.

THIRTEENTH DAY

Be brave!

Mari says that abstinence will make the heart grow fonder.

FOURTEENTH DAY

Today, a Saturday, I put on my sneakers and trotted to the Riverside Park basketball courts. I had all the old feeling of excitement. But I barely got there. My lungs felt like lead. I got shin splints and arch pains and heart heavings so great I promptly had to sit down on the bench outside the fence.

After a half hour of watching, my body throbbed practically not at all. "I can still play that game," I thought, watching a batch of kids play half-court, and in a spasmodic lurch, leaped up.

This was not prudent.

My left ankle scraped rawly against the cement base of the bench. I tripped over my own feet and, falling, caught myself on my elbow. I ripped my pants at the crotch.

Undaunted, I managed to get inside the fence, where the *real* action was. A game had just ended and there was a free ball lying under the hoop. With some effort, and care, I bent to pick it up. My back clicked twice and my elbow hurt. But I took the ball, stepped back half a dozen feet, propelled the thing nonchalantly in the general direction of the basket, watched it fall four feet short, turned, turned red, and walked slowly home.

Mari said she hoped I hadn't played too hard my first time out. I looked a wreck.

FIFTEENTH DAY

Kafka says: "His weariness is that of the gladiator after the combat; his work was the whitewashing of a corner in a state official's office."

I am exhausted, depressed, and, since I have stopped eating apples, constipated again. I read today of an executive who had shuffled himself off this mortal coil from the forty-fourth floor of his office building: he had been on a crash diet.

I have lost all of eight pounds since this mortal combat began. Is it possible that I gain weight merely by *looking at* and thinking about food?

SIXTEENTH DAY

The lousy scale lies. I kicked it viciously last night and have been hobbling like a cripple all day.

The problem is: I have fat cells. And they're poorly trained. They crave food. They convert cottage cheese into pure fat.

Why wasn't I born an ectomorph? A friend of my son, a string bean of an emaciated sort, simply cannot put on weight, no matter how much he eats. The lucky bastard. And I take calories in at the eye!

A Dr. Marci Greenwood has found that certain laboratory rats have an "inherited tendency to become overweight"; they develop high levels of an enzyme before they put on weight. So I have gluttonous ancestors to contend with, too!

But tonight, hobbling onto the scale, noting sadly

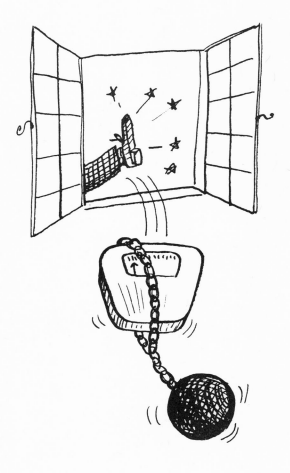

that I had still lost only eight pounds, this profound truth kept twirling in my light head: *Biology is not destiny.*

EIGHTEENTH DAY

My doctor told me today: "Nick, you look like you're bait for a coronary!"

Overjoyed, I said: "You mean I should stop dieting?"

He said: "I mean you should *start.*"

NINETEENTH DAY

My daughter Jennifer came to me in her night-gown tonight, her hair done up in a bun, fresh from a bath. She sat on my lap and said: "O, Daddy. I'd be so proud of you if you *really* got thin."

TWENTY-FIRST DAY

In several hours of televiewing tonight I witnessed color commercials for steak sauce (did they have to show filet mignon with mushrooms sautéed in butter?); ice cream—heaps of it, the size of mountains; soft drinks (four), which made it bubbling clear that I could have no fun in life, and must surely resign myself to quiet desperation, if I did not drink them—and happen to weigh 110 pounds; wine (three); whisky mixes; a slow-dripping spaghetti

sauce—O, terribly, painfully slow-dripping; two ovens with juicy, burnished roasts; a supermarket—

with shopping baskets full of canned fruit, fresh meats, butter, cakes; plump chicken (sold by a man who looked like one); heaps of pasta—a liberal selection, close up, better than that made in Italy, good enough to eat; and—hallelujah!—a feminine deodorant.

Are nuts bad for me? I ate nearly a pound of roasted peanuts while watching television.

They can't be. Look at squirrels.

I told this to Mari and she replied: "Did you ever see a squirrel eat salty roasted peanuts by the pound?"

I told her I had not.

"And when," she asked, "was the last time you ran along branches all day?"

TWENTY-THIRD DAY A curious feeling of lightness and nervous vigor today. My belt came in two notches this morning, my pants feel loose at the waist, my jacket is no longer tight in the shoulders (I had ripped the armpits twice last month).

Beyond that, my eyes, in the mirror, seemed more animated, more alert.

Perhaps these are only illusions. I am surely still heavier than 200 pounds ... no mouse, but the sensations—for that's all they were—are quite pleasant.

Not wanting to confuse the issue, I did my six push-ups and seven sit-ups, and did not weigh myself.

TWENTY-FOURTH DAY Yes, my stomach has definitely begun to contract. All day I feel it pinching in, involuntarily, as if, in labor, I were preparing to deliver something.

I have begun, at night, to do sit-ups and push-ups. They're hell! Especially the push-ups. Tonight I managed a creaky seven. I also simulate jumping a rope, until the whole house sounds like it's got St. Vitus's Dance. How I'd enjoy having some bounce back in my step again!

Encouraged by the looseness in my brown tweed suit, I tried on some old blue slacks tonight. But I could not get them over my thighs. How many summers ago did I wear them? Six? Eight? Ten? Mari says I shouldn't be wearing a tweed suit in July; she has been encouraging me to buy a summer suit. But I reminded her about my old clothes, said I surely would grow too thin for anything I bought now—and anyway, I can't afford to buy new clothes this month.

Sooner or later, probably sooner, the IRS will pull the plug on me. Their little printed notes to me are becoming hostile.

But I am less concerned with them tonight than I am about whether I'll ever get into those old blue slacks again.

TWENTY-SIXTH DAY   The bastard scale must be broken!

TWENTY-SEVENTH DAY   I noted, with some alarm, an article indicating that the churches are on a witch-hunt against fat. One revivalist group stresses the maxim, from John (3:30), "He must increase but I must decrease." A

woman has written a book called *More of Jesus and Less of Me*, and a church-oriented college has expelled a batch of plump students for not losing weight.

TWENTY-NINTH DAY   Anthony, my youngest son, came to me tonight and said: "Dad, will you teach me basketball this fall?"

I told him I thought I could be in shape by then.

He asked: "When are you going to start?"

I *still* cannot do more than ten push-ups and I still haven't broken the 200-pound barrier. On Thursday, I eliminated all but coffee for breakfast; on Friday, I ate barely fifty calories for lunch, eliminating even the cottage cheese from the Lo-Cal plate; on Saturday I had no lunch.

Last night there was a sharp argument between two of my children at dinner. I needed instant energy to solve it and grabbed for a slice of bread, then buttered it. But I held, did not eat, survived the challenge, and felt moral as a saint—only to take a slice of bread with butter and peanut butter after trying to help one of them with his math homework.

Later, though, my weight was exactly the same, 201. I am on some kind of plateau. Is it worth the pain? I may never lose another pound.

O, for a beaker full of scotch, for a dish of cherries jubilee at Teacher's, for a decent breakfast again, for the wisdom of Solomon—for even the cottage cheese on the Lo-Cal plate!

THIRTIETH DAY   When I ordered my broiled hamburger *sans* bun for lunch today, the waitress said, "O, you're dieting."

"Starving," I said, looking at the woman's plump cheeks.

"I know all about dieting," she said. "I could write ten books on it. I'm real expert."

And I listened to her many interesting theories for ten minutes, quite intently, until she said, "I've actu-

ally lost hundreds and hundreds of pounds over the
last few years."

THIRTY-FIRST DAY   I told Mari to buy me a goddam scale that works!
Instead, she gave me a new diet that "everyone"
is on. It demands merely that you eat specific foods
on specific days, in specific amounts, in a specific
order. This is all chemically and scientifically
worked out, she tells me, and guarantees the loss of
ten pounds a week.

Always interested in improving myself, I exam-
ined the miracle diet carefully. Monday and Tues-
day I could manage—if I happened, at lunch time,
to be in a part of town where farmer's cheese and
scallions were served. Wednesday was impossible.

Broccoli.

I had been frightened once by a piece of broccoli. It had been dangling at the end of a fork while
some well-meaning relative, who was quite convinced I could not survive another day without it,
pinched my cheeks to open my mouth. The event,
which took about twenty unforgettable minutes, did
not produce the desired results.

So if Wednesday was broccoli, the diet was out.

THIRTY-SECOND DAY   I resisted the cake at an office party today. Chocolate layer cake, with the prettiest little glazed cher-
ries on it. One is grateful for such minor triumphs.

But there was another printed notice from my
friends the IRS—still a bit more threatening than the
last. I replied promptly to them, for the fifth time and
at great length—and then, pleased with the felicity
of my prose, sure it would stall them for another

month or two, treated myself to three raw carrots.

The carrots were no help.

My mother-in-law, an experienced campaigner in the Weight Wars, says: "Nothing cheers me up like a piece of cake."

Carrots are most definitely not cake.

THIRTY-THIRD DAY

And she took me into Zabar's yes where the Nova Scotia lox lay in pink slabs upon the counters safely behind glass and the garlics strung and clustered yes near Port Salud and Colby cheddar and Danish fontina and Alpsberg Bouille Rondelle Havarti Tilsit and Muenster cheeses and twentyseven different salamis also peperonis all old and ripe and crinkled tawny red and the bolognas link sausages Westphalian Parma Nuss-Schencken Lachsschinken hams honeyed or baked or smoked and roast greasy-

ducks yes special frankfurters turkey breasts liverwurst and pressed apricot rolls apricot levkar apricot jam and bright red candies and nuts in great glass jars and escargots and smoked trout and whitefish and sugared jellies near the halavah yes and chopped liver with shredded egg yes and how I stood so silently and watched trying to meditate on a copper pot dangling above me near the cheeses but could not and the longing that began when I ate with my eyes the sour pickles and the pâté de foie gras with truffles at only thirtynine ninetyfive a pound and the potato salad much cheaper and the glazed pears and sugared pineapple slices and the sturgeon carp caviar eel and the figs from some Alameda garden yes and the basket of bagels yes and the great brown monksbreads yes and the nutcakes and fruitcakes and coffeecakes with their dear little walnuts in brown sugar and why hadnt I wired my lousymouth shut and the cutter giving the fat woman a sample of bellylox the bastard yes and the deepdown longing O trying to think of her at night when she came to me my Mollywife love all love and how love lingered and I saw only pastrami and cornedbeef and petit fours and chocolate lentils and raspberry jelly and goudas and tubs of butter yes and cream cheese yes and marinated mushrooms pickled herring yes and I put my hand out toward the jellied candy bright crimson and lemonyellow yes with snows of sugar on it and I could taste the rare nectar yes and my heart was going like mad and yes I said yes I will . . .
No!

THIRTY-FOURTH DAY   I broke the 200-pound barrier today! Tomorrow I'll *really* start to exercise.

I decided some weeks ago that this affair required a strictly scholarly approach. Books. Research. All I needed to know could be found in the words of the girth-control experts. Dieting was surely one of the most carefully explored phenomena in America, which may say something about America.

And it's probably one of the most lucrative. These diet writers make a fortune. In Thomas Nashe's *The Unfortunate Traveler*, Jack Wilton leaves England because of the "sweating sickness." He reports: "I have seen an old woman at that season having three chins wipe them all away one after another, as they melted to water, and left herself nothing of a mouth but an upper chap." Wilton was a clever, enterprising fellow: he should have bottled the stuff for future generations. There's a fortune to be made in diets, and most of them don't work nearly so well.

But I went to the library and took out a dozen noted specimens of the literature and then, in a bookstore, bought three sure-shot paperbacks and two recent best-sellers and two quickie paperbacks that promised fifty pounds apiece. Since then, between jobs and late at night, I have tried tenaciously to study—and for a while even began to take notes.

Apparently it is possible to do this thing solely on martinis, on grapefruit and eggs, on meat and water, without meat, on only sardines, on lettuce and raw carrots, through confession clinics, at obesity centers, in thousand-dollar-a-week spas, by altering your stomach or wiring your jaws shut. If you believe the books, calories don't count—and count in spades; you can eat all you want—and nothing; you can diet only with hypnosis or expensive analysis, or meditation upon your very own plump navel; exercise helps—and is of negligible help. You can shoot for quick weight loss—or permanent weight loss.

One crash-loss program of pills and spiritual guidance insisted it could burn away fat "two times faster than any diet, five times faster than exercise." Leading medical schools, unnamed, had endorsed it. The program promised to accelerate my "fat-burning metabolism"—did I really have one of those?—and specifically take five inches off my waistline, four off my hips, and three-and-a-half off my ass.

There are salt-free and gourmet diets. There is a no-aging diet, a last-chance diet, a high-fiber diet, a low-cholesterol diet, a high-energy diet, a carbohydrate diet, a macrobiotic diet, a ski team's diet, a pilot's diet, and a banana-only diet. Some people insisted you should eat only one meal a day—in the morning; others said slim was ten teeny-weeny meals a day.

Nor is weight control the only benefit! Higher spirituality may be yours—and "super" sex. Add running to your program and you can transform your life; more cauliflower will prevent fatigue, depression, and every other sin that flesh is heir to. Forget about the gout and gallstones; your heart will become steel; you may very well live forever.

I read the books with all the best intentions.

How much I wanted to find the answers there!

Did I have "poorly trained fat cells" after all? Was my thyroid out of whack? Would I see God if I ate wheat germ? Would I go batty if I ate only sardines?

But alas! The books were quite impossible to read, contradictory, probably dangerous, certainly repetitive; they overlapped and underconvinced. But they were something worse, much worse. They reminded me of Evelyn Waugh's comment, when he met a handsome and prominent lord of whom he had expected much. "He's dull, so dull—so dull.

Oh he's so dull. And you can imagine how much I *wanted* to like him."

The books I read are lethal: their styles pedestrian, terminology obscure, techniques gimmicky.

And the effect of all this reading has not been good. I slipped into the kitchen after reading for three hours tonight, after everyone had gone to sleep, with all the contradictions and taboos and food-food-food in my head, on my brain, and ate three large chunks of salami.

I find more wise counsel in Thoreau than in them all: "A man is rich in proportion to the number of things which he can afford to let alone."

2061592

THIRTY-SEVENTH DAY   Mari wanted to buy something for me, to honor
my triumph at the 200-pound barrier, but I told her
that I did not want "The Diet Computer" from
Hammacher Schlemmer or the scale that lit up.

She finally settled for a handsome white turtle-
neck sweater, which I have begun to wear. I was
deeply flattered: instead of an Extra Large, she
bought a Large.

THIRTY-EIGHTH DAY   Back over 200 again before I went to bed last
night—but this morning I was slightly under again.
Maybe the best way to diet is to get African sleep-
ing sickness. A mysterious business, this up and
down. And all yesterday, starving, I had been so
sure I could *feel* my metabolism chewing up my fat.

THIRTY-NINTH DAY   Since Mari enlightened me about how I was
smuggling in extra calories, I have tried mightily to
evolve a proper diet. I have gone on the simple
assumptions that calories *do* count, that protein
burns fat, that grapefruit juice pinches or contracts
the stomach (at least it makes me not want to eat
anything afterward), that roughage (without salt) is
necessary and "cheap," and that a tart apple a day
will keep me from suffering the anguish of Luther.

A typical day's menu for me has thus been:

Breakfast: half a grapefruit or a glass of unsweet-
ened grapefruit juice; a boiled egg, sometimes two,
without salt; two glasses of water; and black coffee.

Lunch: a broiled hamburger or steak; lettuce and tomatoes without dressing; three glasses of water; two cups of black coffee. Sometimes I take the traditional cottage cheese instead of meat.

Dinner: broiled meat again; salad without dressing again; three glasses of water again; two cups of black coffee again; and a tart apple, eaten very, very slowly.

This Spartan diet keeps me running, and it is as boring as a third-rate prune of a lecturer. But it works.

The chief threat comes at lunch, especially a crucial business lunch. Recently I survived two of them quite handily, with minor modifications. One was at the Harvard Club, where broiled pompano with a bit of lemon helped—and was delicious—until I realized it had been cooked with butter and then, rather gauchely, I sponged it away with a slice of bread. One must be cunning to beat such sneaky cooks.

The other lunch, a Plaza buffet, almost sank me. I had taken three bites of the chicken before I admitted to myself that it was barbecued. Then I survived quite well on four dry slabs of turkey, two quarters of a tomato, four glasses of water, and three cups of black coffee.

All was going swimmingly with my regime, my cunning substitutions, until Mari, who has been peeking into all the health and diet books I bought and following food commentaries in the newspapers with an uncanny eye, informed me that:

1. eggs contain too much cholesterol and I could get heart problems from eating them regularly;

2. cottage cheese, despite its presence on most diet menus, contains too many fats;

3. chemicals in shell foods are dangerous, and some people say you can't even trust a flounder;

4. the caffein in too much black coffee could lead to anxiety, headaches, sleeplessness, irregular palpitations of the heart (all of which I have experienced lately), and, in extreme cases, to death.

I found all of this very sobering news. I was surely in pursuit of health as well as thinness. I did not especially want to bite the dust yet—though there seemed nothing but dust left for me to eat.

Meat. I could survive on that. I loved all kinds of meat, even without sauces, even broiled. Meat had been my mainstay. Sunflower seeds were a possibility: Mari had been pushing them lately, leaving them conspicuously around the house. But I considered these a last resort. Water. There was always water. It was safe, devoid of morbid calories, even (after a fashion) tasty.

Then Mari said, rather too merrily, I thought: "O, here's an article by a prominent doctor that claims the meat producers are pumping cows full of hormones to make the meat redder . . ."

Fine!

". . . and it may lead to cancer."

I had been worried about meat for other reasons. Meat and water, together, in ample quantities, produced the greatest immediate weight loss: high protein and a flush mechanism. But Lamar Underwood had told me at lunch one day—while the bastard popped some french fries into his mouth and sipped his third martini—that the meat and water diet worked wonders for about a week at a time, and then hair would begin to grow on my nose.

So I was left with sunflower seeds and water, and perhaps a bit of unred meat now and then, and I was having an extremely spare lunch today with my remarkable friend Sparse Grey Hackle—an eighty-five-year-old gentleman who still comes to work every day—when Sparse said: "What are you doing that for?"

I had been drinking my seventh glass of water. It was pure and cold and, in its way, quite delicious. "Diet," I said.

"It's not healthy, Nick."

"Sparse, there's nothing left. I've eliminated all fats, all salt, all sugar, all bread and starch, eggs, cottage cheese, meat (except in minuscule portions, as you can plainly see). There's nothing left. I must have water!"

"Do as you like," the wise old gentleman said. "Do as you like, of course. But in my day we had a saying: 'Water at meals leads to an early grave.'"

FORTIETH DAY

My seven or eight glasses of water a meal are causing me a little inconvenience. At one restaurant you have to tip the gentleman in the john; the old guy could retire on what I paid him yesterday for five pees within an hour.

Worse is not finding a john.

This is especially a problem when you've left the restaurant too soon. It has led to my keeping a special two or three pages in my notebook listing strategically placed johns around the city. I do not rate them. A john is a john is a john in my condition. It's merely essential to know where they are. There are beauties in the Hilton and the Plaza if I'm in those areas. All coffee shops do *not* service this need and must be cased first: it's nearly fatal to zip into one, order a pro forma coffee, drink half of it in a lurch, and then be trapped without a john. Design Research has one on the third floor but when I raced up the three flights a week ago I knocked over a shelf of glasses. I've got two helpful spots in the East Eighties, there's Grand Central Station, of course, and I'm covered in the West Thirties. I made a great find two weeks ago in the East Seventies, and have used it regularly, and the Westbury, ten blocks south, has one on the main floor but you have to go through the bar and a rather haughty maître d' greets me with a scowl and now merely points: he knows I am there to give, not to receive.

FORTY-SECOND DAY Tolstoy says that when he was a boy someone told him to go into a corner and *not* think about a white bear. He could not do it. Nor can I, in my perpetual corner, *not* think about food. Since I *must* think about it, I have been perfecting techniques for rendering the white bear harmless. Often I glare it down; several times, in restaurants, I have ordered a low-calorie meal and it has come out with such sinful side dishes as french fried potatoes—which I bring to my lips, then put carefully, slowly, back on the plate. This shows my absolute superiority over food.

In the donut shop today, my eyes locked to the bin of strawberry-filled donuts, I tried this mantra: "I am looking at a specific strawberry-filled donut. It is a delicious donut. I enjoy thinking that someone else will buy and enjoy this enjoyable strawberry-filled donut. Someone thinner. Someone who has earned this donut. I have not. I believe in my heart that if I eat that enjoyable strawberry-filled donut, which I can almost taste, it will cause me to suffer cancer of the left testicle."

This worked beautifully—until the sales clerk, hearing my harmless little mantra for the third time, asked me politely to leave.

FORTY-SIXTH DAY

All day, a Saturday, I have been remembering meals past. This pleasant activity, which took up most of the afternoon, was intended as a continuation of my spiritual exercises.

I took two tall glasses of pure cold water into the living room about two o'clock, while the children were out, and had a good think about Botin's in Madrid, which Hemingway in *The Sun Also Rises* calls "one of the best restaurants in the world." I thought of how I had met Gonzalez, from my Army post in Croix Chapeau, and how we went there together one night and ordered roast suckling pig that came with tall decanters of *rioja alta* and sautéed potatoes. The skin of the pig was the burnished brown of horse chestnuts and the meat was soft and moist and we ate too much of it and drank too much wine and enjoyed ourselves into a stupor. Later I told Mari's gallery owner about Botin's and about how much Hemingway and I had enjoyed it, thirty years apart, and she went there and got stomach poisoning and had to be carried to her plane on a stretcher. You could write a story about that, and about other great meals in Spain, but no one would read it.

That memory had taken a bad turn so I began to think of the magnificent Tour d'Argent in Paris, where I had once gone with Sandy Bing. He had asked me whether I wanted to eat "comfortably," and, dummy that I am, I had said, "Sure. Who wants to eat uncomfortably?" We were in Paris on leave and I had bought a French suit that day for about $11, a black corduroy that looked quite arty on the rack but proved less than practical. On my way to La Tour d'Argent, the buttons popped on the jacket, and when I saw the restaurant—especially the dining room, high above the Seine, with floor-to-ceiling windows and no fewer than three waiters in tuxedoes at every table—I wanted to bolt or at least to eat in a shadowy corner.

There were none.

Sandy chose a table in the dead center of all that elegance and I decided, "This is Paris and they may well think I am a brilliant artist being treated by his patron," and clutched my jacket, to hold it closed. I kept my winter scarf wrapped around my neck because they demanded a tie, and my hands cupped and high in front of my chest, like Bogart in *The Petrified Forest.*

I felt a bit stiff but the meal was remarkable: pheasant under glass, pâté de foie gras, creamed asparagus, wild rice and a choice vintage wine, Margaux.

I drank a lot of Margaux, which made me think of the W.C., and I must have eaten too much for midway through the meal the waist button on my trousers popped (I had not wanted to wear my

Army belt, thinking it inappropriate, so wore none) and then the buttons on my fly popped, too—all five at once.

One of those three tuxedoed waiters kept hovering behind me—filling my wine glass, replacing the butter—so I crossed my legs. This helped not at all. And then one of the pheasant bones managed to disengage itself from the plate and slip down through the opening in my pants and work its way down my leg.

I had to go real bad now but Sandy wanted to stay, comfortably, and have a brandy Alexander with his strawberries and I could not find the words, in that awesome room, with him eight feet away on the other side of the table—I could not find the words to explain why I was anxious to leave or excuse myself but did not want to stand up alone.

Finally I insisted we *had* to leave and, when he had gotten up, took a position directly behind him and trailed him closely (to his bewilderment) until we got to the street, whereupon I raced down to the shadows of a quai near the Seine.

That memory was tainted, too, but when I dozed off I had a positively spiffy recollection of a rougher meal Mort Seaman and I had had on a fishing trip to the St. Lawrence. I felt us coming off the windy river at noon, and saw again the warm farmhouse on the Canadian side, and the heaps of food that were brought in to us at the cherry-wood table— platters of roast chicken and steak, bowls of french fried potatoes, fresh salad with a rich creamy house dressing, warm home-baked rolls with tub butter, and finally the hot blueberry pie with strawberry ice cream.

I could taste it.

If there were false fat, like a false pregnancy, I'd have gotten it.

As it was, I woke with a start, felt starved, and nabbed two or three slices of apple and strawberry pie before I quite realized the dream was over.

Alas. The days when I could eat meals like that were over forever. Quite gone.

And I knew, as I trudged back to the living room to do my fifteen push-ups and twenty sit-ups, that a middle-aged man must be ever vigilant.

FORTY-EIGHTH DAY   A marvelous, glorious day. I feel that I could diet forever, climb Everest, try out for the Knicks (who need me). Have they ever had a forty-odd-year-old guard? I'd be an incredible draw, an inspiration.

My friend Abdula, the Black Jewel, greeted me this morning on my way to work, saying: "Nicky. The incredible shrinking man! You look twenty-two!" He was wearing a pink beret, had been up to some mischief all night, and wanted to rap—and I wanted to rap with someone who said I looked twenty-two. He said he was going to Al Roon's gym for a workout and steam bath and I told him I was thinking of signing up, to put the finishing touches on my metamorphosis from plump cockroach to lithe young man with dreams intact. When I told him I had once been one of the best light-bag punchers in the world—and could play "The Star-Spangled Banner" on the light bag—we began to spar and he asked if I'd teach him and I said I would and I felt twenty-two and 150 pounds again.

Then, in the office, three people said they did not believe it: I could not possibly be the same person. It had happened overnight. But I should buy a new suit—that old tweed looked perfectly baggy on me.

I could not have gotten a sweeter compliment. In fact, the suit *is* hopelessly, happily, too large: it

slides at the shoulders, you could carry a baby kangaroo at the waist; even the trouser legs are for an elephant. What a marvelous feeling this gives me, and almost enough courage to try on those old blue slacks again.

I needed only half a grapefruit for lunch, with two glasses of water and one cup of black coffee; I felt stuffed to the gills. I tried but could not remember how I ever ate so much before.

I have decided to wear this old suit another week, then, when I hit 185, I'll junk it. There is no sense having it altered; I won't be 185 for long, anyway. I'll be 175 the week after that, and who knows whether that will be the end? Why not go all the way, the whole hog? Maybe 165, or 150 again, and stabilize there. In fact, why be a piker about it, show false caution? There is not a reason in the world why I should not stabilize at 135.

Is there a Guinness world record for this kind of thing?

There must be some kind of award—and surely I deserve it.

I feel holy, beyond threat. Nothing can turn me from this sacred crusade any more. I could comfortably lose 100 pounds by Christmas, or Easter at the latest.

Still, maybe I won't be able to stop. Maybe I'll contract anorexia nervosa. My grandfather once told me about a catfish he trained to stay out of water. Each day he kept it out a bit longer, until it became terrestrial. Then one day it fell off a bridge and drowned.

My constipation continues, and is a pain.

Now that I can do twenty sit-ups and fifteen push-ups, perhaps I should start playing basketball again.

FIFTIETH DAY

A touch of the flu or a cold today and I promptly hit the icebox with all my former fury, devouring everything in sight. This has happened several times before. I'll get a sudden spell of fever or chills or lethargy or depression and will resort to food—as if I have been programmed to do so. It's safer than alcohol and drugs and infidelity. It's safe, so safe, and O, so cheery.

But surely I can survive these threats without having to eat bread and butter, chunks of salami, cake, and—may no one ever know!—strudel. Three pieces.

FIFTY-FIRST DAY

A devastating afternoon with my tax accountant. He says he thought I had paid last year's taxes. I reminded him that I had written the IRS what by now are seven long explanatory letters—outlining in great detail my current financial position, the mountains of work I was doing, my expectations. I reminded him that I had told him about this and I asked why the IRS had not had the courtesy to reply to one of them. Not one.

Now I have their notice that I must cough up within a week or appear before them and give good cause.

I asked my accountant if he would *please* come down with me—I could not face them alone—but to my amazement he refused. He merely said:

''There's nothing I can do for you. You've earned a lot and you've lived beyond your means. You'll just have to pay the piper.''

I feel abandoned, helpless. There's a great lump of hatred in my heart, the size of an avocado, that says: ''The graduated tax is the most pernicious of governmental liens on your purse and soul. Legalized gangsterism. I am being penalized for holding all those jobs, for wrecking my health, for working harder than my neighbor.'' There were days, while I earned last year's income, when I gave guest lectures at 7:00 A.M. in Spring Valley, rushed back to New York where I was executive editor at a complex book-publishing house, rushed up to the college to teach a full load of courses, then rushed home to work until 3:00 or 4:00 in the morning on some ghostwriting assignment. I ate constantly, to keep up my energy, to stave off depression. I ate hot dogs on the run, between jobs, in subways; I piled heaps of food near my desk late at night, when my head kept nodding.

And all the while I had not realized that I had this silent partner, surely in cahoots with my tax accountant, waiting to bankrupt me.

Yes, bankrupt. Worse: I owe the government more than I can possibly scratch up in a week, even if I sold every piece of furniture I own. If I could only have until the end of the year, until January.

Will there ever be an end to this pressure?

When I got home I ate everything in sight—two apples, the entire dish of cashews and almonds, a raw carrot, an orange, about fifty wheat thins. If I am to be brought to the brink of financial ruin by the IRS, at least I would go there on a full stomach.

Then I collapsed completely and started in on the chopped liver and salami and yesterday's spaghetti and meatballs.

I now weigh 182, a tremendous achievement—but I feel all the gains to be highly precarious since this setback. The meeting with my silent partner will be the ultimate test.

Falstaff says: "If I do grow great, I'll grow less."

I want merely to grow solvent.

FIFTY-THIRD DAY

To consolidate my gains during this difficult period, I have made up a careful list of what not to do. I am being driven by the IRS back to food but I shall resist with all my power and ingenuity.

1. Try to reconcile my bank statement
2. Go into Zabar's
3. Play chess with my children
4. Do homework with my children
5. Watch the Knicks play basketball
6. Watch food ads on television
7. Have business lunches
8. Grade student papers
9. Listen to the news or read the newspapers
10. Read diet books
11. Meet with my tax accountant—or think about him
12. Remember meals past
13. Shop with my wife
14. Think about how much more weight I must still lose
15. Think about the ineluctable fact that I cannot have another strawberry shortcake for the rest of my life
16. Breathe?

Still, with a bit of Spartan discipline, all may not be lost.

FIFTY-FIFTH DAY

Two good days. I may yet survive this horrendous ordeal.

FIFTY-SIXTH DAY

A slight regression at lunch today when, at dessert time, someone at the table mentioned taxes. But apparently it was not too damaging. I weighed 185 tonight.

FIFTY-SEVENTH DAY

I meet with the IRS in three days.
May the gods bless and protect me!

SIXTIETH DAY

All is lost! I have abandoned all hope—beginning with this wretched diet. This will be my last entry.

I appeared at the IRS office this morning as ordered, without the support of my moralistic, priggish, smug tax accountant, and sat for an hour on an empty stomach along with the other sad offenders. Finally I was called into a small glass-enclosed booth by an illiterate young man who mumbled that, "moneywise," I must pay up immediately the thousands I owe, plus penalties and interest. I told him I had written seven long and very patient letters to his superiors, explaining my situation in meticulous detail. I produced the carbons. I told him with great courtesy that I would have appreciated a reply.

"Have you got the money delinquent?" he asked.

"No," I said. "As I explained, I've been in debt for more than ten years. When I got the money last year, after working my balls off for it, I paid my debts."

"It weren't your monies for paying no one."

I became livid. My stomach began to rumble. "I earned every penny of it!" I shouted. "I earned it working eighteen or nineteen hours a day, for weeks at a time. I nearly killed myself. Can you understand that?" My voice kept rising; my stomach began to speak. "Look, I have no intention of *not* paying. I only want a little time. I do not think it's fair, I do not like it, but I will admit I owe the money. I owe it to you. I just want a little time. A peanut's worth of time. Can you understand that?"

"Can you pay or ain't you going to pay?"

"I'm going to pay. I'm going to pay every cent I owe you guys. I just want a little . . ."

"You ain't going to pay now?"

"No," I said quietly. "No. I can't. Not now."

"Miss Winch," he said. "I think you'd better talk to Miss Winch."

"Who's she? The chief lemon here?"

"She is the chief here. Yes."

While I scuffed my shoes against each other and chewed off a loose thread from my tweed jacket, he phoned and a few minutes later Miss Winch came in. She looked thinly at me, then at a folder of papers about my case. Though the folder did not include the letters I had written, I was astounded at the amount of information this government, which I hardly knew, had about me.

"Fill this in," Miss Winch said, handing me a printed yellow form, the color of macaroni. It asked for an enumeration of my assets. I breathed deeply and began.

No stocks. No bonds. No real estate. No savings account. A piano (which had belonged to my wife's family). Five fishing rods.

"We don't care about those," she said, looking over my shoulder.

I started to tell her that they were Paynes and
Dickersons, worth a great deal—and that the value
was sure to increase. I wanted to show *some* substance. I thought of how I had used those rods on
glorious rivers, and how pleasant and simple it was
to be on a river, fly fishing for trout. But I did not tell
Miss Winch this. Somehow I did not think she
would understand.

Minimal furniture. Thousands of books. My wife's
paintings.

"Does she sell them?"

"She did but we had a fire some years ago and
all her old work was destroyed, every bit of it. You
should have seen those stretchers hanging tilted on
the walls, with their guts burned out."

"What are they worth?"

"Well, she's been looking for a gallery but
they're hard to find. The art world's very faddish
right now. Tight. Hard. Hard as undercooked stew
meat. Still, I'm hopeful. And she's very devo—"

"She doesn't sell them regularly, these pictures?
They haven't a fixed market value?"

"No. Not right now. But she's exceptionally tal-
ented, a peach of a painter, and . . ."

"Forget the paintings."

"They're her *life*. She . . ."

"Do you own a car?"

"Look, she's really a tremendously fine artist and
you're insulting her, and in school she . . ."

"Do you own a car?"

"No."

"Any *hidden* assets?"

"My soul."

"Don't be cute!"

She looked over the sheet, shook her head sadly,
and told me to sign it. I wanted to sign it immediately, to do anything that would end this business

and get me out of there. Would they let me go if I
signed it? Would that be the end of this inquisition?
I was acting like an idiot and they were idiots but I
could not sign without reading the document, and I
told her this and began to read the last paragraph.

Suddenly my eyes blurred, my stomach was a
whirlpool. The last paragraph said, in effect, that if I
did not cough up the money I owed within ten
days, my silent partner could come into my house
and take or sell *all* my property, including furnish-
ings and personal belongings—even my Payne
and Dickerson fly rods. My silent partner could put
liens on my salary and any other earnings, fine me,
and even clap me in the clinker.

I would not sign.

"You have got to sign," Miss Winch said. "You
have no choice." I noticed that she had a prominent
brown moustache, exactly like the one on the prune
of a headmaster at the boarding school I'd been
sent to when I was four. I looked for webbed fingers.

"Can we talk about this?" I asked. "I'm a good
citizen. I teach at a city university—I'm a very devoted teacher, really. And I have a large family—
family man—and I've worked hard, as hard as a
one-armed chef for the past fifteen years, and I've
always paid my taxes, every strawberry of them,
and all I want, all I want is a little more time. *This*
time. I can't tell you how important it is to me."

"Good citizens," Miss Winch said, smiling, "paid
their taxes in April."

"I *am* a good citizen!" I shouted. "I may eat too
much, I may *look* prosperous to you, but I'm a hard-
working family man, a damned good citizen!"

"Don't shout at me, Mister."

"I am *not* shouting!"

Why hadn't my tax accountant come? The glass

walls of the cubbyhole were closing in; I was being forced to the pit. Miss Winch, with her moustache, was a foot from my face, coming closer every second; Moneywise was leaning on his elbows now and learning how this was done. My stomach began to howl; my throat developed an erratic twitch. I had visions of pizza and strawberry cream cake.

"Now, I respect that you're a professor and probably a very high-type personality, but moneywise we must have this settled at once." Did they all learn English in the same cesspool?

"I can't!" I said, my voice straining. "I have no money. None. You can check."

"I am very sure," Miss Winch said very slowly, still smiling, her face an inch or two from mine, "that a very high-type personality like you, with a steady job at an important university, can *borrow* the money."

"I've spent ten years paying off the banks. Do you know the interest they charge? Fourteen percent. Maybe more. Usury. They're criminals. I *can't* start in with that again. I can't!"

"I told you not to shout at me, Mister!"

"Damn it!" I muttered.

"Did you damn me, Mister?"

"No. *It.* Can't I have another mouth? Month. *Month.* Two mouths. Two would be much better. *Months.*"

"You've had since April 15, when the good citizens of this country paid their lawful taxes, their fair share, and moneywise we have seen nothing from you whatsoever."

"I told you—or did I tell Moneywise?—I've written *seven* letters. Seven. They were very long, very literate letters. Here. I'll show them to you. You can read them yourself. No one answered them. No one had the goddamned courtesy of a pizza-schlepper to . . ."

"I think you had better sign that document this instant, Mister," Miss Winch said forcefully. "Otherwise, the penalty could be a severe fine or imprisonment or both."

I looked at her, my chest heaved twice, mightily, and I found myself urged up out of my chair. I grabbed the pen, looked at it, looked at Miss Winch and Moneywise, squeezed the pen mercilessly in my fist, and plunged it down to the bottom of the document, scrawling my name.

Then I raced out.

Down the elevator and into the street I kept seeing her smile, and I felt my stomach pound and pinch. I needed a fix. I'd have given anything for a food-fix.

And when I found it, at the pizzeria two blocks north, I fell—O, how I fell.

TWO

Triumphs (of sorts)

I am wearing my good old brown tweed suit regularly again and it is only a trifle loose in the shoulders, at the waist. The disaster led to total abandonment of the diet. I am too embarrassed to detail the past three months.

But today I have quietly but formally started to diet again. Though I did not gain back every loss, I am a shade over 200 again, still a few pounds ahead. If I learned anything from that two-month binge of self-abnegation, it is that I must change my life, not merely my eating habits. And I have slowly begun to do that.

My new tax accountant—a solid, patient, psychiatrist of a mathematician—is much help. And so is my recent departure—at his suggestion—from two of my jobs. Thoreau is right again. The problem with the John Field family of Baker Farm is not their poverty but the way they lived.

Under my new scheme I will spend less and therefore have to earn less and therefore will not need to share so great a percentage of my income with my silent partner. I have also immersed myself in my own work—reading and other activities *I* choose to do, have long wanted to do, and enjoy—and find myself thinking less about food (since Christmas dinner, at least), and nibbling less. Food is really a damned dull route to salvation.

I have chosen this the convenient first day of the new year to consolidate my efforts and start again. It is orderly, neat, to start on January 1. My resolve is quiet but firm. I shall eat less and eat carefully (some of your best friends will smuggle salt into a salad) but I *shall* eat—and eat most foods. The hysteria is gone. I will do this thing and do it right. I will exercise regularly and eventually play some basketball again. I like that game and have no intention of seeing it vanish from my life.

My one current worry is that nagging lawsuit a woman has brought against me—after one of my sons hit her with his bicycle three years ago, when he was twelve. I'm still not sure it was his fault, and I've grown doubtful whether we should have left our name and address, which had not been asked for at the time. The case has become worse—and more complicated—than Jarndyce v. Jarndyce in *Bleak House*. She's suing me for $500,000.

That's a lot of bread.

JANUARY 15

These past two weeks, whenever I mentioned that I was dieting again, to friend or stranger, I inevitably got one of several responses, all of which contain some snippet of truth:

1. The person, who you notice is plump, says he has been dieting for most of his adult life and is thus an expert on the subject; he is on The Perpetual

Diet. The principal ingredient of this diet is a healthy dose of preoccupation with it. The person thinks of nothing else, knows nothing else; there is no room in his brain for anything else. He is constantly losing weight, making genuine progress, and is always plump.

2. The slim person who once weighed forty pounds more says she is the only successful dieter she knows.

3. Yawns.

4. Recipes—you always get recipes.

5. Stories—inspirational and grotesque.

6. Apocalyptic comments on the age and how it is unique in its ability to promote the acquisition of blubber.

The Jeremiahs blame fat on technology. There is a superabundance of food, brought by modern transportation. The pilgrims had a 600-calorie Thanksgiving of succotash, johnnycake, and corn-meal bread; we manage to consume some 5,000 calories on the day of the big bird. Also, science has created a vast array of processed foods, which hunger and fatten where most they satisfy. Philip Wylie, in his marvelous essay "Science Has Spoiled My Supper," refers to certain frozen vegetables as "hairnets simmered in vaseline." Such food lacks nourishment and fails to satisfy our aesthetic needs. So they say.

Technology also leads to tension. One impulse from the vernal wood calms us, or once calmed us, but today we are mostly surrounded and bombarded by noise, smoke, drabness, tension, machines we don't understand, cab drivers of vulgar tongue. "Civilized man," said Emerson, more than a century ago, "has built a coach, but has lost the use

of his feet. He is supported on crutches, but lacks so much support of muscle."

But surely it is more personal. Thirty to 50 percent of the country may be overweight, but in each case I suspect that somewhere behind all the fat lies the sure knowledge that one is less than one might have been, ought to be, can be. The magazines, the ads, television shows push success. It is all around us and it is a big hype. So we think ourselves dumber than we might have been. We think that we have not used our talents wisely or well. We have traded on our talents in ways that are sinister. We're not good enough fathers. Or husbands. Or wives. Or lovers. We eat out of disappointment. Food is a pacifier. No one understands us; romance has been lost. We eat because of these frustrations, then become even more frustrated because we are fat, lethargic, listless, unable to fit neatly into a Brooks Brothers suit.

A rather ferocious businessman told me on the phone the other day, explaining why he had acted toward me in a sharkish way: "That's why I am where I am." I have avoided that ambition which feeds on others, and always will, though somehow, through a bizarre sublimation, I have fed too heavily instead on food. I don't want men like that to chew on me, nor do I want to chew on them, nor do I want to hear the sound of my voice change to their jungle snarl: but food is not the answer.

What did a pizza ever do to me?

JANUARY 19

My mother-in-law called from Florida this evening. She was concerned by my report that I had started to diet again. "You don't know how to diet," she told me. "*I* couldn't take weight off that way, and if I did I wouldn't keep it off." She knew. She had been dieting for years. She'd "been through them all."

But she wasn't dieting anymore. What was the sense? Unless you were truly obese, most doctors (she said) did not worry about a few extra pounds. Anyway, nothing cheered her up, she told me three more times, more than a piece of cake.

JANUARY 25

"The scale must be wrong," Mari announced this morning.

"Ah, ha! So you know what it feels like now," I said, gleefully. "Gained a pound or two, eh?"

"No," she said. "Lost three pounds. Can't understand why. Do I *look* thinner?"

Then I remembered. I had adjusted the scale down the night before, to see what it would feel like to weigh 185 again.

JANUARY 26

Lunch with Lamar today. He remarked that I was a Yo-Yo. Up and down.

I told him I was on the way down, permanently, this time. "Each person has to diet in his own way," I said. "And I've found a sensible pattern." I began to tell him about moderation and good sense and the delicious ratatouille Dorothy made, with boiled rather than fried vegetables.

"I know how *I* could diet," he said. He was eating veal scallopini with mushrooms and wine sauce, munching his fourth piece of bread, nibbling olives, sipping his third martini. He'd gained ten pounds since I had seen him last.

"Give me five months," he said. "Just five months."

"I'll bite. What would you do?"

"I'd go to a spa," he said. "I'd go to a very special kind of spa." And he went on, in great detail, describing how they'd get him up every morning at 5:30, give him a good rubdown, lay out a scientifically balanced meal for him. Then a little tennis. A light lunch. A little golf. Another rubdown. A light, specially prepared dinner in the evening. Early to bed.

"You'd grow floppy ears and turn into a donkey," I said.

FEBRUARY 1

I am astounded at the tenacity of that lawsuit. Today my lawyer calmly informed me: "I would be remiss not to warn you that your $100,000 insurance policy might not cover the settlement. If it goes over that amount—and it now looks as if it might—they could take everything you own."

"The boy said she was walking against the light."

"Juries like little old ladies with white hair, not vigorous young boys."

"Will you come to that examination-before-trial with me and the boy?" I asked.

"I'll try to make it," he said. "The insurance lawyer will be there, and I'm not expert in negligence cases like this."

"The examination is in three weeks. Don't you think you ought to come?" Somehow I did not trust the insurance lawyer, whom I'd only spoken to on the phone.

"I'll try," he said.

FEBRUARY 5

I was always a reluctant fan. Give me any old thing to do—tie a trout fly, throw a ball, fuss with some words—and I will prefer it to watching. But one of my boys is playing high-school basketball this year and I have become a rabid fan.

Watching him, everything in me becomes alive, tense. I project myself into his every move. Yesterday, in the first game of the play-offs, I found myself up and out of my seat a dozen times. Then, in the fourth quarter, he stole the ball, dribbled down court, drove between two men, and went scudding along the floor and into the wall. One of them had tripped him. I saw it. But the referee called my son for charging.

Charging?

Impossible!

I found myself urged up out of my seat and shouting hoarsely at the "blind, stupid, asshole" of a ref. I was in the middle of the court, maniacal, my back hunched forward, words spluttering out of my mouth. I'd never been like that before in my life.

The referee turned sharply to me. "Get," he said, with fiercely quiet deliberation, "off," with force and low venom, "this court this instant."

I did.

Perhaps I had better give some serious thought to playing myself, to a long-delayed return to the court. I have no safe future as a fan.

FEBRUARY 15

Slowly I am beginning to lose weight, devour less. My body, if not lithe, feels much less cumbersome. It is responding to the diet in a downright friendly way, almost as if it *likes* less food. Anything with calories looks sinful, nauseates me. I weigh myself only once a week now and my records show 194, 192, 187, 185.

I realize more than ever the importance of exercise and several weeks ago began to convert flab—the product of *sitzfleisch*—into muscle. This is not an easy task. Those planned standard exercises—like sit-ups and push-ups—bore me almost as much as diet books.

But I want to tone my muscles and have been poking around to find the right ways. I like to jump rope—there is a rhythm and grace to it—and have begun to do this, along with simulated rope-jumping at night. In the spring I'll be able to fly-fish again, and will be sure to walk more then. I've been getting out of the bus a few blocks before my stop, then walking the rest of the way home. I try to walk a little faster than usual.

But my mind, always, turns to basketball—the great game of my youth.

Is there anything left?

Can you really return at my age?

So this weekend I began to play a bit with my sons, Paul and Charles: their greatly improved skills and strength, my utter exhaustion. Still, there may be a few games left in me. How I loved that game, and love it still.

How good it was to be back on the courts, flooded with memories, feeling, every now and then, a touch of the old fire.

FEBRUARY 20

Another call from my mother-in-law, who has been in the hospital for a cataract operation. She says she met a seventy-three-year-old woman with a gorgeous figure; the woman's daughter is a nutritionist: they both eat wheat germ and drink vegetable juices and look like models.

"She looked terrific," my mother-in-law said. "Svelte. Ten years younger than her age. And her daughter did, too. But then I learned that she had diabetes, gallstones, and a touch of the gout. I don't need that. I'd rather eat cake."

MARCH 1

A traumatic three days with my lawsuit!

I appeared with my son, fifteen minutes early, for the examination-before-trial. The Municipal Court is a dreary place—a place where futures are decided in gray, drab rooms. No one but Fleischacker, the woman's attorney, looked pleased. He was a peppery, weaselly, quick-talking, always-smiling man. The victim had blue-white hair, walked with a cane, and seemed born to charm juries.

My attorney never appeared. I had called his office five times during the previous few days, giving all information about the meeting, asking him to appear or send someone else—and definitely to call me back. I heard not a word from the man— and he has now gone the way of my first tax accountant and is free of me and my embroglios and cheap cases forever. A lawyer representing the insurance appeared; but he wasn't from the company itself: he had been hired only for the day, for this examination. He was a stupid, cocky, loud bully of a man in a loud sports jacket, and he had heavily greased hair and flashing teeth. He had not yet read the original brief on the case and did so, in no more than four minutes, in front of me, the pages flashing like his teeth.

"So," he said to the boy, scrawling some clumsy lines on a sheet of paper, "you were driving your vehicle up this street, toward that one, with the light, at 3:22 P.M. on the afternoon of July 20, 19 . . ."

Three and a half years ago! The boy had been twelve. I was sure he could not remember a detail of the scene.

"No," I said. "I don't think those are the right streets. He was riding up Thirty-seventh. Look, I don't think he even . . ."

"I'm talking to the boy, right? Do you want me to help or not? It was this way, right? *Right?*"

The boy looked at me and then at Flasher. Flasher took the boy by the shoulder, confidentially, and started to walk with him down the hall. "Right? Right?" I heard him say.

"Yes," said the boy.

The man was talking rapidly and walking rapidly; he had been ten minutes late and Fleischacker had urged him to hurry. We were in the heart of the hallway, walking through heavy, noisy crowds. Flasher had his arm tightly on the boy's shoulder now and had gotten some distance ahead of me. He was walking quickly and talking quickly: I could see his head bobbing up and down, and I could see my son's head nodding. I began to skip, then trot. I felt sweat on my arms and on my face. I came up close to them and could hear the man talking about streetlights and the position of the woman and I knew in my heart that the boy remembered none of it. I felt bands of tension grip and claw my chest.

"I didn't ask you!" Fleischacker said, ten minutes later. We were in a minuscule gray room, the five of us seated around an old table, a stenographer in the corner taking down every word on his little machine. The elderly lady with blue-white hair had not said a word, nor had she looked at me.

"But . . ."

"Look, mister," said Flasher. "Don't say *one word* unless you're asked."

"But he wasn't. . ."

"Not a word!" said Flasher.

"I re—"

"Is he going to shut up?" asked Fleischacker. "Or do I have to speak to the clerk?"

Flasher leaned toward me and said: "Do you want me to handle this? Do you? Do you want me to help you or not? You're jeopardizing the case. The company won't pay a cent if you gum it up. Do you know that? Do you?"

Why hadn't *my* lawyer come?

Perhaps he still would.

Why hadn't I eaten lunch before this inquisition?

On and on it continued, the boy agreeing with whatever Flasher (who had not even read the original deposition) said, contradicting himself, plowing on, trying to do the right thing, remembering not a word of the original deposition, having no clear image of the accident itself, watching the old woman, looking at her cane, nodding "No" to Fleischacker, who kept grinning and leading the boy deftly into further errors, trapping him like some dumb rabbit in a snare.

Every time I tried to interrupt, he cut me off—no, he did not want *my* lies, *my* fabrications: he was after the *truth*. Which was what? I did not know. The boy did not know. Flasher did not know. There were no witnesses. Fleischacker did not know. He had probably persuaded the woman to sue in the first place, since we had only heard of the case six months after the accident, when we'd all forgotten about it.

The truth?

It shall make you free. The truth shall make you thin! The meal shall make you calm. These lawyers shall make me bankrupt.

And then, suddenly, it was over and I had been

invited to say nothing, only to reaffirm that I was the boy's father, that I had bought him the bicycle, that I had taught him how to use it.

I walked silently out of the room with my son, my arm lightly on his shoulder. Both of us were still dazed. When we were outside, I asked if he wanted a sandwich. He did not. I was starved. I bought two apples from a pushcart dealer and gave one to my son. He ate it slowly, saying nothing. I ate mine slowly, too, as we walked, my arm on his shoulder again, to the subway station.

That night, sitting together after everyone else had gone to sleep, he said: "I couldn't remember that day at all, Dad. I thought the lawyer, our lawyer, really knew the facts so I said what he told me to say. I shouldn't have trusted him, should I, Dad? There are people out there you can't trust, aren't there?"

Then this morning the call came from the head legal honcho at the insurance company: the case was settled. For $67,000.

"What a figure!" I told him, pleased it was finally over, pleased it was under the $100,000 face of my policy, but astounded by the figure—for a bike accident involving a twelve-year-old boy and a woman who might well have been off the curb, against the light, looking to me for her pension. The hazards of modern life were unbelievable.

The lawyer told me the testimony was full of contradictions and impossibilities; there were no eye witnesses on either side; she had her cane and blue-white hair and we had a boy who was robust and athletic. We had no case.

But $67,000!

What a close call.

To celebrate, I took Mari and the boy to dinner

tonight, and I talked to him patiently about all that had happened, and what it meant. There was much to be learned from it all.

I had a large salad and treated myself to a few shakes of salt, to give it a bit of taste. I had come through unscathed, without breaking my purse or diet. I hoped my son would be as lucky.

MARCH 10

Though I know I should take up golf or tennis or racquet ball or Ping-Pong, I am continuing to play, tentatively, my old game, basketball.

I had made several stabs at this ten, then seven years ago. Something always popped: a tendon, an elbow, one of the four fingers I botched playing baseball in the Army. Now I am back in the park, on the cement courts, trying again.

How I love basketball!

"You're in your mid-forties, Nick," Mari warned.

"I think I can come back," I said. "I want to *feel* my body again; I want to *materialize* after all that ghostwriting I did last year; I want to wake up all those old fiery urges."

"You're crazy."

I said: "I think I can do it. I think I can come back."

She said "Fat chance."

MARCH 15

I have had a few fallings-off.

Occasionally, in my zeal to see results, I have dieted too hard. The result: extreme dizziness, eyes heavy and hollow, radical nervousness. At times I have treated this diet like Martin Eden lusting after the total use of his time and energy. He worked nineteen hours, then found he had to cut back to eighteen and a half. I sometimes eliminate break-fast, reduce lunch to merely grapefruit and coffee. The results, inevitably, are a food splurge, a raid on the icebox, secret munching.

I must try to remember that you cannot train a fish to live out of water nor a man to live without food.

Always, I have tried to return to a sensible diet as soon as possible, and I have managed to do that.

And I have been trying to become more conscious of a necessary equilibrium between mind and body. When I played basketball and weighed 150, I didn't think; when I began to think, I became unconscious of my body—and it blew up in my face. What we are dealing with here, as none of the diet books have realized, is Augustinian dualism versus Thomistic reconciliation, or what a harried hack can do to sew together a torn life and regain a dram of dignity.

I got into those old blue slacks today!

MARCH 17

Reading a biography of Melville recently, I found this reference he had made of Emerson. "His belly, sir, is in his chest, and his brains descend down into his neck, and offer an obstacle to a draught of ale or a mouthful of cake."

This is a puzzling comment and I am not sure what it means; but it sounds as if Melville found Emerson too *heady*, which he was. Cake and ale would seem to epitomize an earthier life than Emerson was capable of; unlike Whitman, who wanted to chew up the whole world, like a cow munching grass, Emerson thought too much and didn't eat enough.

Yes. I must be careful of such asceticism, that Spartan, niggardly, nibbling attitude to life.

MARCH 20

A pleasant day of spring and anything seems possible.

In Michigan, in the depths of winter, I remember that the streets froze so solid with ice and packed snow that you thought no amount of heat, ever, could melt them. The snow was piled in hard heaps along the curbs and was packed solid on sidewalks and roadways. Even on particularly bright and hopeful days in January and February, none of it disappeared. A silver sheen, a wetness, might come to the top of the packed snow and ice by lunchtime, but it would freeze solid again by midafternoon.

Then slowly, however solid it appeared, the slight turning of the season, the constant application of increasing heat, would make itself felt. The piles of dirty snow along the curbs—like rolls of fat—diminished; the streets became merely rutted with ice, then streaked, then filled with rivulets of flowing water. The true frame of the world, in its original skin, appeared. Little bumps began to appear on branches that once were covered with layers of ice; then buds; then bright flashes of an old remembered green. By late April, you wondered how you could ever have doubted that the snow and ice would ever melt. You looked forward to increasingly warm days; you fished in rivers that, each day, lost more muddy snow runoff, more of their bloat: they grew clearer, lower, closer to the shape they were meant to wear.

I have melted into the high 170s and can taste triumph in this little battle.

MARCH 25

With my increased activity at the courts, several friends have warned me to go to a "stress clinic." There, carefully tested, I can be instructed on my capacities and limitations.

There are "physio-scan mini-stress" tests and moveable electrocardiograms. There are special sports clinics and nutritional counseling services. Everything is tested: blood, lung function, pulmonary function, circulation (by an ultrasonic doppler), metabolic function, and posture.

I'm sure it's a terrific idea, but a lot of people don't have $400 to put into a disease they don't even have yet.

APRIL 12

This will be the longest and most melancholy entry in this melancholy journal. It closes a chapter in my life.

Some weeks ago, encouraged by my weight loss, I made those few furtive walks to the Riverside Park basketball courts, and this led to renewed hopes and renewed dreams of that time when I weighed 150 and lived only for the hoop.

I had bloomed late. Though I had not played any high-school ball, I fought my way onto the freshman team at the University of Pennsylvania, past recruited ballplayers and men who had made all-state in high school. And then I spent three long years on the varsity as a sub-sub, my chief pleasure watching Ernie Beck, my friend and classmate, make All-America and lead us to the Ivy League championship in 1953. Dick Harter, who later became such a superb coach, was on that team, too, always talking basketball—and I remember Dick Dougherty's wise

body-wit and Don Scanlon's jumper, some extraordinary left-hand drives by Bobby "Kangaroo" Brooks, Timmy Holt's lithe speed, and the day Howie Dalmar arranged a scrimmage with the Minneapolis Lakers and Slater Martin scooted around

Vern Mikkelson and Jim Pollard and George Mikan and made me feel as though I had two broken legs and blurred vision.

Ernie used to pray and cross himself in the locker room before each game—and then get twenty-five points. I began to pray for Howie Dalmar to put me in. It didn't work. Once, when we played on television, I dribbled down court by myself, in those familiar last two minutes when all the subs go in and chaos reigns, and threw the basketball neatly over the backboard.

I finally won a full letter in my senior year, and the Bill Wollman Award for the Best Junior Varsity Player (though there wasn't a JV then); my name is still on a plaque in the Palestra. But in my entire, dubious career I scored only three points. All on foul shots. All at Dartmouth, during Winter Carnival. I had given the game every ounce of will and passion I could muster but at 5' 9", with no high-school experience behind me, I had not gone nearly so far as my colossal dreams dictated.

But in the Army, in my early twenties, I suddenly came into my own, a couple of years too late.

If only Howie could have seen me burn up the league in western France that year!

At 148 pounds, just out of basic training, I could touch the rim easily, average twenty-two points a game, and lead a no-bench team from the dingy little post at Croix Chapeau to a divisional championship at Bordeaux and into the All-France play-offs in Paris. That had been a double-elimination tournament and we had played SHAPE first, a team of ringers collected by some egomaniac sports colonel. They had two guys who later made All-America (one of them 6' 6"), an ex-Globetrotter, and a kid 5' 8" who jumped center and could dunk. We had no one taller than 6' 1".

When they went through their pregame warm-up,
we stopped our own shooting and merely watched,
wide-eyed.

But we pressed full court, the five of us, and
hustled like mad the entire game, and we beat them
by a point in double overtime. I scored thirty-five
points. It was the high moment of my little career.
My eighty-yard run. And I wished with my heart that
Dalmar had seen it.

(After an interminable night in Paris, we comfortably lost to SHAPE two days later by a mere 53
points.)

When my three boys were small I used to tell
them about those good old Army days. On a long
noisy trip home from the country, I would tell the
one about our winning the regional championship

by taking three games in two days. At first they were awed and quiet. Later, when my weight rose to 195, then soared blithely over 200, Paul and Charles would interrupt:

"We *know* how you once won three games in two days, Dad."

"And how the games were played in a field hangar . . ."

". . . that was so dark you couldn't see the ball under the baskets . . ."

". . . and so cold they had heat blowers at half-court."

I would say: "They really did. Big, red heaters. At mid-court."

"And how you scored seventy-six points . . ."

"Seventy-eight."

". . . in the three games, all played within twenty-four hours. One the first night, two the next morning and afternoon. And how the opposing fans would trip you if you got too close to their sidelines, and spit on the cement floor of the hangar, and the refs never saw any of it."

"Did it *really* happen?" asked Anthony, my youngest, his eyes wide; he had only heard the story four or five times before. "Just like that?"

"Just like that," I mumbled. "Many many pounds ago."

But as the years went on, I wondered. There were no witnesses I could summon to vouch for my brief hour of glory. All that remained, of all those desperate, passionate years of hooping, was the faded scroll that announced I had been awarded a varsity letter in 1953.

My most vivid memories, which I now shared with no one, were of half-court ball at Wingate Field. It had been a whole world, the only world to me in Brooklyn, before I went to Penn, with its regular cast of characters and its own patois.

In our park we had Natey, George, Herbie, Stanley, the Commissioner (I never knew him by any other name), Hooks (nor him), Artie, Ira, Mike, and the Marine (who looked it, always wore fatigues, and rarely spoke). We played in the dead of winter, carrying our own shovels to the park and clearing enough space to play—the cold so sharp our lungs heaved until we coughed and gagged, our frozen

fingers too brittle to manage a ball. We had a joke about those guys like George who had one unbelievable push shot, banked from the right side: that he practiced all winter with gloves and came down at night and shot for hours with a candle on the rim. He was lethal from his one spot. And from no where else.

The pole was attached directly beneath the backboard, and you could not take a truly hard driving lay-up without either crashing into it or grasping it as soon as the ball left your hands, and then swinging around it like a monkey. People new to the court rarely left unscarred after an afternoon of ball with us, both from their own untutored moves and because we ceremoniously used the pole as a pick. I had only two serious confrontations with the pole: once, on a desperately determined drive, my knee went into it and turned to jelly for a month (I made the shot); and once my forehead met it squarely, opened like a can, and had to be stitched that afternoon.

Whereafter I returned to the park and still managed to get in four or five good games before dark.

"Nobody quits," we would say on a dreamy June afternoon after twenty or thirty hard games, which had begun about eight in the morning and been interrupted only for a popsicle or two from Sam's pushcart for lunch. "Nobody like us, like the *real guys*, ever stops playing basketball. Nobody ever kicks the habit."

"Yeah. Who'd want to?" asked George.

"I'll play till I'm eighty," I said.

But even before I went into the Army, there were defections. Several of the older boys went into business and of course were not seen at all during the week. On weekends in November when the trees were sere and the games were hottest, they were pale portly remnants of our older heroes, snuggled into loose topcoats from which protruded dress slacks and dress shoes. One of them even began to smoke a cigar. I remember watching them that fall—three, four of the regulars—sitting on the bench outside the fence, caged away from all that was life, talking, kibitzing about a move or shot, remembering perhaps, never playing.

Did it finally come to *that*?

I felt closer to a guy named Schnaiter or Schlotter who was twenty-six and had tried out for the Knicks for five years running, though he'd never played college ball. He was a ball bum, an addict, and he's probably at Wingate to this day, hooping merrily. I was at Penn then, a tenuous last man, but that did not keep me from vaguely wondering now and then whether I too should not try out for the Knicks some day. I was still improving and Wat Masaka could not possibly last forever.

But something unfortunate happened to me during my last months in the Army. My Wharton training flagged and I fell in love with the word. I began to read. First Maugham and Jack London. Then Hemingway—O, a lot of Hemingway. Then Kafka,

Dostoyevsky, Yeats, Donne, Faulkner, Baudelaire. Jane Austen. Rimbaud. Melville. That kind of reading. And I did it with far more intensity than ever I had brought even to half-court. And when I went back to school for a Ph.D. in English, suddenly,

somehow, mysteriously, basketball was gone. Poof.
I was years behind and there was time for nothing
but reading—Nashe, Browne, Joyce, and Proust
now, Morris Croll on "The Baroque Style in Prose,"
nasty delicious Waugh, Pushkin and Goncharov

and Babel—dazzling, athletic minds—and then marrying, fathering, and all those jobs, jobs that tore into the passion I had fanned with such a fine and fresh fury.

And suddenly I was past forty and over 200 pounds.

Poof.

My three boys had all taken a liking to the game, and for several years I had gone to the Riverside courts to watch them, and even, in my mid-thirties,

I'd attempted to make a brief comeback, halted when I fell on my right elbow, which promptly popped a lump the size and color of a plum. Strange. My body did weird things now. All my old finger fractures started to swell up, my ankles were as brittle as candy canes, there was no rubber left in my arches, and I would get sharp, deep pains in my chest.

But there seemed a little left, a few good moves. And how I still loved the game—the rhythm and force of it, the blurring, twisting sensuousness of it, the speed and quickness of a drive, fake, spin, and shot.

I wondered if Ernie was still playing, how much *he* had left. I had last seen him in a pre-season Warrior game in Poughkeepsie: in the locker room, having his ankles untaped, he told me of the tours he had taken that summer, how many games he had played. He smiled when I told him, for some reason, that I was currently passionate about a guy named R. M. Rilke. Beck looked weary to the bone.

The names had changed but many of the same types were at the Riverside courts: a bell-shaped waddler with a lethal one-hand push—or heave; a guy who habitually played in dark glasses, a blue shirt with a little alligator on the breast, and pointed suede shoes—and had an incredibly long, seemingly off-balance two-handed shot that only occasionally missed: we had had one like him, too. Half a dozen players had those curiously defined stances and shots that characterize the pathological half-court player: a ball shift in midair and then a left-handed shot (and practically no other discernible talent); a magnet *only* from the left corner.

The one full-court game was dominated by big, lean, highly competitive men, eighteen to thirty, who played regularly and with all the flair and speed that have come to characterize the best of the city game. They were strong, agile highleapers, and often hard-mouthed. "It's a tough game, little man," one said to me the day I tripped and went over on my elbow. God, I'd have loved to be nineteen or twenty again and run with them all day.

But I was past forty, and only slightly regaining a few scraps of the past. I did not especially want to play Dick Diver in front of my oldest sons, who were getting sharper on the courts every day.

Several times I went down early on a Saturday or Sunday, to practice alone. When I played, I was sure to choose a court with fourteen-year-olds or old-timers, and to use my head more than my body. The hardest part was remembering what I once could have done—and seeing how paltry was the music that I could wring from my aging instrument. Now and then someone would jock me—make two or three effective, scoring moves, block one or two of my shots—and I would feel that fierce competitive drive burn like acid in my brain and I would want to let out the wolf, take on the guy with all my force, chew him up.

But I held back. Always I tried to smile and let my man have his day. I had had mine. Briefly. Long ago.

Today, a gorgeous day in mid-April, a day all at once cool and calm and bright, I decided to check myself out, good and proper, on the courts. Alone. At midday. Perhaps there was something left.

No one would be there, and I could see exactly how much was left of the famous Lyons double-pump, the jumper, the quick moves I had always depended upon. My fingers were stiff but usable; my chest still hurt, but only when I breathed hard. Green buds were fuzzy on the park trees, and limberly I skipped and scuffed my feet a few times on the way down to the park, whistling, like in the old days.

The four courts were deserted.

I left my bush coat on and began close to the hoop—lay-ups without dribbling, short turnaround jumpers, a left-handed hook, a few wrong-side twists from underneath. I remembered Septembers at Penn and the same ritual and the huge hopes I would always have for each new year.

A few shots went in but there was a heaviness in my arms, a stiffness in my fingers. I moved out a few feet and tried a few more jumpers. Short. Too hard. A little to the side. There wasn't much of a touch left. Maybe they had raised the rim. I seemed farther from it on my lay-ups, farther than I'd been that year in the Army—four, five inches from the rim now.

I took off my bush coat and flexed my shoulders back hard several times. I jumped up and down for five minutes on the balls of my feet, to loosen my arches. I tried a longer jumper and nearly tripped over my feet. I tried a few old moves—faking once, twice, then sweeping right, toward the basket.

Maybe there was a *little* left to work with.

Maybe.

I felt a bit of power in the turn, authority, some of the old quickness. Double-pump then up, under-hand, softly. *Yes.* Dribble out to the foul line, fake, jump, the ball held high, higher . . . *yes.* Another jumper. *Swish.* And another two. *Swish. Swish.*

The body remembered something.

Fifteen minutes of that—making more and more shots, having the sweet satisfaction of watching a decent percentage go in now, feeling the hard-earned grace recalled in arm and leg—and I knew it was still possible to enjoy this thing that had been my youth. I began to look for a couple of guys to play with. *A little hoop, a little b-ball.* My children would not be out of school for another two hours. There was now a two-man game in progress on the end court but it did not look like much. Another hour of practice would be best.

A lean twenty-year-old with a moustache came over and began to shoot with me. He had a fair jump shot. Then two more young men came over—one 5' 10", about 180 pounds, built like a soccer player; he kicked the ball a few times, bounced it off his head, and I knew he was. The other was high on something. We shot for sides and I got to play with the guy who was high, and to cover the soccer player.

Something is going to go, I thought suddenly. *The fingers probably.*

The soccer player was all over me, fouling me, waving his arms madly, having a splendid time pounding the hell out of me. I did not call a foul. In the old days I rarely did. It slowed down the game.

I played tentatively, trying a fake, seeing what my man would do, letting my insanely wild teammate shoot the first five shots. They were all slammed against the backboard; only one even touched the rim. Our slim opponent dropped five one-handers in a row; he was a ballplayer.

I made a short jumper, then a left-handed lay-up, then a delayed pump. I got a few rebounds and felt my body grow hungry for harder play. I elbowed the soccer player away twice, slipped behind him and stole the ball, played weasel-quick. Not much of a game, not very good ballplayers—but I was enjoying myself. You have to learn to work within your limits, that's all. It was not even a game in which I would have played in the old days, but I was moving deftly now. I could score at will against the strong and awkward soccer player, without press-

ing too hard, without embarrassing him. No need to do that. I set up my teammate twice: he made one of the shots, from underneath, all alone, on a pick-and-roll worthy of the name. He had not seen where the ball came to him from. Even my passing was getting sharp.

The lean opponent dropped two more jumpers, the soccer player sent one flying from half-court, two-handed, and it swished. He tried to ram into me on a drive but I side-stepped sharply, dipped behind him with my right hand, and, without touching him, stole the ball. Twice I outpositioned him under the boards and, though he jumped on my back, I scooted away with the rebound.

There was not *something* but a lot left. The chest pains were not too severe, my ankles were holding. I was slipping into the rhythm of the thing.

Swish. Two more: one jumper, one drive from the left. The soccer player whammed me but I made the shot anyway. And we won.

I sat down on the green bench outside the fence, pleased with myself—sweating profusely but damned pleased. I was in the game again. I could still do this thing. I would weigh 165 in a month and then I'd be able to regain even more of what I once had.

The courts began to fill up now. The regulars were arriving for the full-court game. I watched them: a couple of 6' 4" black guys; a blond seventeen-year-old I had been following all spring; a guy with a wild Afro, about 5' 8", who dunked; Mel, a slim young black who put the bite on me for fifty cents again; Dick, a football player, in from college. They jostled one another under the boards for a free ball, took long one-handers.

Not for me. Not any more. They were too young, too strong, too quick, too aggressive. Enough. I had

had one good game. My boys would be down in an hour; I could watch them. I could be that much of a fan. And I could remember.

"Holly—woooood!" Mel said, making one of his strange, long one-handers. "All right, you mothers. A little ball. Les' play a game. I din' come here to shoot. Les' play."

I got up from the bench to retrieve my ball. It was not the best there and they would not need it. As I came around the fence, another ball bounced toward me and I took it, dribbled once, and shot. *Swish.* "Holly—woooood!" shouted Mel, nodding his approval to me. "All right, these two here beeg mens choose 'em up and we play a little bas-ket-ball."

I found my ball among those dropping with alarming regularity now, then walked toward the gate. They were choosing up sides and Mel had taken charge. I turned to listen to his quick patter and heard him coach one of the captains: "Take that there little white feller. One with the curly hair. There. He's sma-*art*. Smart ballplayer. Per-fessor. I'm a per-fessor, too. I per-fess. I con-fess. I de-press and jus' press."

The man motioned me onto his team.

Well, if Mel really thought I was worth picking I ought to give it a try. I hadn't played so badly before. I could run with them, full court, for a half hour. With Mel on my team we would at least be in the game.

Two minutes into the ballgame they gave the ball to the smart player. He was all alone on the right side, took a quick step after bobbling the ball, and jumped for a shot. Someone, he never knew who, swatted it cleanly into the fence before it had gone an inch. Two plays later they gave it to him again. He was, by now, panting wildly. All the old will to

win was back in him. He drove for the basket,
bobbled the ball again, took six or seven steps, felt
like a perfect asshole, and was properly called for
walking. He noticed that he who called the walk
was Mel, who was therefore not on his side but the
other.

Euchred.

I was the dud. The lemon. I knew it now and so
did everyone else on my team. And on the other
team. They huddled and my man, the lanky seventeen-year-old, left me completely on defense and
double-teamed my team's ace, a lefty with springs
for arches. On offense, the kid took me right into the
pivot twice and scored twice, quite quickly.

Someone muttered: "Turkey."

*But I played with the great Beck. I'm the only guy
here who played college ball. In my day I could run
rings around all of you*, I thought, getting my second wind, then my third, working my way into
position, calling for the ball, hustling back on defense, stealing the ball on their fast break with a
move I had learned from Timmy Holt, then losing
the ball, moving always without the ball (since they
appeared determined, now, not to let me touch it).

*Two jumpers and I can salvage this disaster. A
good double-pump, like the old days, and they'll
know who I am. Like that time in the hangar, when
the French shouted, Comme ça un danseur.* And
that's what I had been: graceful, lithe, a fantastic
leaper. Once. *Hang in. A little longer.*

I looked to the sidelines, now packed with on-
lookers. My children weren't there. Neither were
any of their hoop friends, who would have told.
Neither was Dalmar.

I heard the word "turkey" again, and blanched.
Ten to eight, theirs. We could still pull this one out,
and in the second game I could come into my own.

I knew I had enough left. I knew I could still play in this league. I had played with Beck!

"Holly—woooood!" shouted Mel, making his fifth straight shot from nearly half-court, dancing, clowning afterward.

I felt a twinge in my left leg. Nothing to worry about there. I had never had problems with my calves. When I went, it would be an ankle, or the chest (which hurt not at all now), or the elbow again, or the fingers. Probably the fingers.

Up and back. Up and then back down again. Our left-handed ace was keeping us in the game with his long jumpers. The score was sixteen a-piece. We could still win.

We?

My opponents' opponents were playing with four men. They didn't see me anymore. I was racing back and forth, diving for the ball, calling for the ball, playing a sort of butcher-shop defense, now and then taking the ball out, but never being given the ball when there was the threat that I would do something like shoot or dribble, never past half-court.

Then it happened.

Quickly. With finality.

I leaped with all my might for a rebound, fully ten feet away from the ball, and felt the muscles tear and the sharp, splintery pain in my left leg.

I put my foot down ever so gently and collapsed. I could not support myself. The pain was so excruciating that I could hardly hobble to our nearest man and beg him, in a cracked voice, to get a replacement. He had been a poker-faced, hard-nosed, un-smiling player the entire game. He wanted nothing more than to win, as I had once—with all my heart—wanted to win whenever I played. He looked slowly down at my leg, supported gingerly by my big toe, and a broad smile spread rapidly across his face. Replacement? Sure. Sure. He'd get a replacement. It would be a pleasure.

I was done. Probably for months. Perhaps, at last, forever.

It took me an hour to walk the eight blocks home. I clutched the basketball in my left hand, against my body, and flexed the perfectly limber fingers of my right. I saw nothing but the pavement in front of me. Each step was hell. Every curb was an Everest.

At least my boys had not been there. Perhaps I would take them to Philadelphia some day and show them my name in the Palestra. That sounded like the safe kind of thing a retired old hooper, looking for a moment of the past regained, ought to do.

The courts were surely "no country for old men."

APRIL 20

Still confined to the house. When I heal maybe I'll take up squash—or Ping-Pong. I used to be damned good at Ping-Pong.

What about bocce?

Hell, I'd probably bust my fingers playing chess. It's a fragile life.

But I will not let biology become destiny!

APRIL 21

I have begun to read like an addict again, the way I did that first year in the Army. Pure pleasure. And safe! No calories.

The cost of food, I'm told, has gone up 10 percent this year. So, reading and not eating, I am making a small fortune.

APRIL 25

I have been rummaging around for a new sport, some form of exercise suitable, appropriate, for a man of my age and obvious limitations. I have begun to hear of the miracles that running performs—for brain and soul as well as body.

Yes, running promised everything: health, weight loss, muscle tone, spiritual highs, even more "brain power." A young friend quoted me a passage from a best seller on running about that brain power and I had to tell him that, though I did not run much and did not think I ever would, for brain power I preferred Mozart, Dostoyevsky, Aristotle, Chaucer, Kafka, Kant, Rilke, Marquez, and a couple of hundred others who probably did their marathons in a thousand installments.

Trout fishing is an abiding passion but I once calculated that you burn up a measly 123 calories in an average day of fishing—about an egg and a quarter's worth. Piff.

With my leg still brutally painful I ought to think more in terms of pitching horseshoes.

APRIL 28

This evening Mari and I ate at one of those restaurants with a free shrimp and salad bar. I had a small portion of salad with a little vinegar and no salt. Honorably, I also put no croutons and no shrimp on the plate.

At the table next to ours, quite close, sat three divas—robust, meaty, hungry divas. No mice. When we came in, one of them allowed that she would have a third portion of salad—with chick peas, pickled beets, shrimp, croutons, and blue-cheese dressing. When she came back to the table, the other two got up and allowed that they would have third portions, too. Soon all three were munch-

ing away, engaged in some positively serious eating. After a few minutes, they began to talk, mostly at
the same time, mostly in loud, full, resonant voices.

First they talked about fishing, so my ears pricked
up. All three divas loved to fish. They especially
liked to fish with food. One angled for catfish—
"hungry little beggars"—in Florida, with chunks of
greasy salami; the others preferred carp fishing with
a special formula of bread, honey, and chicken
blood. How the carp loved the little bread, honey,
and chicken-blood balls! It was so much fun to
watch them, down on the bottom, nibble at the bait
with their round little mouths.

Mention of nibbling seemed to stir in the divas a
desire to talk about food. They began a lively dis-
cussion of what *they* were hooked on. They all
loved pasta, all kinds of pasta. They all loved
sauces—thick, rich, heavily seasoned sauces, with
lots of garlic and salt and hot peppers. They all
loved French pastries, Italian pastries, Viennese
pastries, Broadway cheesecakes, *any* strawberry
cream pies, all seven-layer cakes—"And, O, have
you ever tasted the strudels on East Eighty-sixth
Street?" The other two had indeed tasted the strudels on East Eighty-sixth Street, many times, O,
many times, including two days ago.

"Keep your mind on your vinegar," Mari said.

I whispered: "That is a fascinating conversation."

"Sort of one-sided."

"It's making me hungry."

"Everything makes you hungry."

"Nonsense."

"Stop leaning in their direction."

"If they order cheesecake," I said, "I may not be
able to resist."

"Yes we will."

"Yes," said the grandest diva, wiping her mouth,

thrusting her broad shoulders back, wiggling her mighty jaws. "Yes, there is nothing like really good pastry for keeping up your weight."

"Of course not everyone sees it that way," the youngest diva said. She shook her head and *her* jowls wiggled too. "Some people today are prejudiced against weight."

"Bigoted."

"Narrow-minded."

"They've been brain-washed. They simply do not know any better."

"Absolutely."

"Nick," Mari whispered, "don't listen to any more of that rubbish."

"Have you seen *Vogue* magazine lately?" They all roared and one of them put a hand to her forehead and shook her head, which truly was quite ample.

"Skeletal little girls. Do people really think *that's* beauty?" Sneers. "Poof. They need a good meal or two. There's nothing to them. All bones. And they are positively not healthy-looking. Sickly, really. Drained. They look like . . . that Vela girl looks like she needs . . ."

"Cheesecake," said the grand diva. "Lots of cheesecake. I'd make that little girl eat cheesecake every day for a month. She *could* be a pretty thing—but there's nothing to her."

"Just bones."

"I'd give those rock singers some cheesecake, too: puny girls with puny voices."

"It's the American obsession with dieting. That's what causes the problem. Why, I couldn't even get a size 38 blouse at Saks last week. It's never been this bad. Obesity! The word was invented by the press. It's a cheap, stupid, petit-bourgeois prejudice; that's all. Look at the women in Rubens's paintings!

Those are *real* women. Round arms. Round cheeks. Some bosom on them. There's a certain symmetry, a certain fullness . . .''

"They're gorgeous, darling."

"The point is, there's something *there*. There's some meat on the bone. In every thin girl there's a good fat woman crying to be let out."

I whispered to Mari that they might be right. Perhaps this long trek of mine, this shrinking, this painful fight with the bulges, ounce by morbid ounce, was merely an illusion, a sad mistake.

She booted me under the table. Hard. In the shin.

But I was not convinced. Hadn't an English friend told me of a man who had gone on a strict grape-fruit and steak diet and dropped from 14 stone to 13 to 12 to 11 to 10, and then started to eat again. But he kept losing weight. Lots. No matter how much he ate. He'd had to be hospitalized for a month—*to put on weight*. It was a serious problem. Anorexia nervosa. The phenomenon intrigued me. One psychotherapist, Steven Levenkron, blamed precisely this "Twiggy image," this lust—pushed by the fashion and advertising worlds—to be "super-thin" for the cases that came to him. Sometimes he'd get calls from new patients and the voice would seem to say: "I don't deserve any space in this world; that's why I'm so small." I told Mari that this anorexia nervosa was a serious matter.

"Not for you," she said.

"Anorexics get hospitalized for months. They have to be fed intravenously. Sometimes they just vanish; they could die. It could happen to me."

"That'll be the day."

"Yes, you've got to work to keep your weight up," the grand diva said. "It's not easy sometimes. Sometimes you don't feel like eating"—she had finished her third salad ten minutes ago and was

deeply immersed in a gigantic bowl of spaghetti—
"but a person *owes* it to herself to do so. Maybe I'll
have a few more shrimp, Carla."

"You haven't said a word to me in fifteen minutes," Mari said somewhat later.

"I was thinking. Maybe they're right."

"Bull."

"I'll take the cheesecake," said the grand diva to
the waiter. The others ordered cheesecake, too.

"I'll split one with you," I said to Mari.

"No you won't."

"Waiter . . ."

"No!"

"Waiter, I'd like . . ."

"Cantaloupe!" said Mari. "Two. With lemon."

"Shit."

When the divas had disengaged themselves from
the table and left, and I had scraped my cantaloupe
to the hard rind, I leaned back, lit a cigar, and said
philosophically: "Those women really enjoyed
themselves. And in a world of many options, perhaps theirs is a viable alternative position. Don't
knock it. I've been thinking . . . maybe the world is
perishing from an orgy of self-denial. Maybe . . ."

Mari said: "Cant-a-loupes for diff'rent folks."

MAY 1

As an experiment, purely in the interest of art, I went on a deliberate two-day binge. I wanted to determine precisely how much weight I would gain back if ever I abandoned my new vigilance.

The answer is: five pounds.

Would you believe it? In two days a watermelon sprouted in my stomach.

Astounded, I got on the scale a second time, checked the figure, got off, stepped on and off five times more, and went downstairs to tell Mari.

"I see," she said.

"I've learned immensely from this," I said.

"Once an artist, twice a glutton," she said.

MAY 3

I signed up at the "Y" today and, when I entered, I noticed a really bulgy fellow on the scale, fiddling with the balance weights.

He apparently did not like what he saw, because he frowned and marched off to the steam room in a huff.

After I had changed into shorts and a sweat shirt, I saw him back on the scale again.

And then, after my light workout, I saw him on the scale still again.

And after I had showered he was on it again, then back to the steam room, then, when I was ready to leave, back on the thing again.

Mystified, I stopped to watch him and edged to within several feet of the scale.

He got up on the honest old indicator slowly that last time, as I had done many months earlier, when I was beginning my diet. Then he adjusted the balance weight to 170. Good grief! Did he *really* think that's what he weighed? Had he tried to lose twenty pounds in a steam room in one afternoon? Impossible. Like the "nigger" of the *Narcissus* trying to force his head through a knothole. But it was so. He began to nudge the weight to the right, pound by pound. He did so with great care—176, 177. Then he pushed a bit harder, to 185. That was a bit more like it. But not enough. Then he pushed still harder, and I saw his shoulders sag in resignation, and then he slammed the two weights back and stomped off again to the foggy oblivion and delusion of the steam room.

MAY 6

Though I still hobble on my shredded tendon, I have been dieting well, consolidating my finances, beginning to exercise with moderation in the "Y." And, having lost another three pounds, I have begun peeking at myself in mirrors, "courting an amorous looking-glass" with curious regularity. This morning, looking closely at the pinched cheeks and boyish shoulders, I found myself saying,

"What is your substance, whereof are you
    made,
That millions of fair shadows on you tend ..."

and had continued to

"Describe Adonis, and the counterfeit
Is poorly imitated after you ..."

when I shook my head at all this adolescent narcissism, laughed at the handsome, smug face in the glass,and went downstairs to do my thirty sit-ups.
    The truth is, I am growing in favor with myself. And the feeling is not half bad.

MAY 8

The Encyclopaedia Britannica gives no clue to the importance of the grapefruit. It includes a brief paragraph on its history, outlines the fruit's characteristics, describes a few of its twenty-odd varieties, and has a few comments on its culture and production. A superficial treatment.

The grapefruit is the dieter's best friend. Too many paeans cannot be written in its praise.

From personal use, its benefits seem to be several. Of general importance, it provides substantial quantities of vitamin C—and I have had no colds all spring. Numerous learned commentaries suggest that, when combined with a high-protein food such as boiled eggs or lean meat, it produces a reaction in the body that actually burns off fat. From my experience, this appears to be true: the strict use of a high-protein food and grapefruit, even over a period of only several days, definitely produced the quickest weight loss. Beyond that, though, the grapefruit seems to curb or satisfy appetite. A half grapefruit—with its tangy, slightly sour taste—before any meal, will induce you to eat less. It may even contract the stomach.

The grapefruit should be eaten slowly, the spoon gouging out every bit of the globular meat; done as a ritual, very slowly, this will take you quite as long as it takes your dining companion to eat her pâté. You will feel you are participating in the meal fully—which mere juice precludes.

A grapefruit late at night, when, all around you, your children are munching cake, is better than an apple and will comfortably carry you through the night, after which, for breakfast, another half of grapefruit will give you that finely sour taste and tang that properly slaps you awake.

Buy a dozen. Take them to work. Take them to play. Write poems about them. They're so potent that I sometimes think I can lose weight by merely looking at that pink or yellow fruit.

I ate one an hour ago—and it tasted so godawful I haven't wanted to put anything in my mouth since.

MAY 9

I threw out the last of my fat-man clothes today, burning my bridges.

MAY 15

I noticed several times during the past few days that Mari was eyeing me in a new way, a way I vaguely remembered from long, long ago.

"You're lighter," she said.

"You think so?"

"I can tell. Positively."

"How?"

"Come upstairs, Nicky."

So I investigated the look thoroughly and found that it was backed by pure lust.

O, brave new world that has such passions in it!

Good-bye, Fosco. Good-bye, great Falstaff. Good-bye, Laughton and fabulous fat man, Greenstreet. Good-bye, strawberry shortcake. Good-bye, pizza. Hello, irresistible Attic form!

JUNE 1

"What's that?" Mari asked, looking over my shoulder.

"That," I said soberly, putting the last touches to my brilliant diagram, "is a Fat Consciousness Device. I want to leave some permanent contribution to the world, based on what I've learned. This diet wasn't just for me, you know."

"No?"

"It was for posterity. Now watch how this will work. It's positively brilliant. Hammacher Schlemmer could sell a million. Might solve our few remaining financial problems, too."

"Hammacher Schlemmer sells approximately *one* of each Rube Goldberg device they carry."

"Sears, then. Look. When the subject, me, raises high-caloric food to his mouth, it must pass over this electronically sensitive mechanism in the arm of the chair. This causes a fist installed in *Jennifer's* chair to punch her sharply in the ribs. Now what does Jennifer do when she's punched in the ribs?"

"She blames Anthony and screams."

"Right! And what does Anthony do?"

"He denies everything, says he's being falsely accused, and slams his fist down on the arm of his chair."

"Perfect. A small computer in Anthony's chair is keyed to the telephone, which promptly rings, which makes me put the food down. Then, whoever answers the phone is told that I'm wanted. I go to the phone and receive a penetrating shock, and then a voice says in a high falsetto . . ."

"You're crazy!"

"No. It says . . ."

"You'll have to do it without devices, Nick. You'll have to keep the weight off because you *want* to keep it off. So will everyone else."

"You think so?"

"I know it."

"Maybe. Maybe you're right. But don't you want to hear what the falsetto voice says?"

"Not particularly."

JUNE 4

I have been wondering whether the discipline of dieting is transferable to other functions—scholarship, business, figuring out what to say at a cocktail party. It's not. Dieting merely encourages you to think more about dieting.

JUNE 6

I am nearing the end of this long journey and have watched myself—in utter shame—fish around constantly for compliments. Do I need such regular confirmation? I've already gotten more than a hint of what's in store for me now. But today I positively would not let Mari go shopping until I heard it from her mouth.

"What do you want me to say?" she asked, reaching for a check I had just written for her.

"You might, just possibly, say something, have *something* to say about the way I look."

"You look fine, very fine. Now can I go?"

"Is that all?"

"Yes," she said, in desperation, "you've lost some weight."

"Lost *some* weight? That's all you can say to me?"

A shrug.

"Isn't there anything else you'd like to tell me . . . about the way I look?"

"No," she said, tapping her fingers. "Nothing."

"Nothing!"

"Nothing."

"Nothing will come of nothing!" I said sullenly,

retrieving my check and putting it back in my pocket. "I've had a monstrous year—or didn't you notice? I've nearly starved myself to death. And I did it all for you!"

"Nonsense! You did it for yourself, which is why you should have done it. And you did not almost die; you're more alive today than I've seen you in more than fifteen years. You're almost the size you should be now. You look pretty good. Not bad. I'll settle for you like this—if you promise with your heart that you will never, ever, ever let it come back."

I took out the check, handed it to her, and said, with deepest sincerity: "It will come no more. Never, never, never, never . . ."

"Just play it straight," she said. "I'm bored, bored, bored with food and food jokes. O, so bored. Can't we maybe talk about books or plays or paintings again?"

JUNE 8

What Mari said makes good sense. One must think less of food even more than thinking of less food.

Hawthorne, describing the old patriarch in the Custom-House in *The Scarlet Letter*, says: "His gourmandism was a highly agreeable trait; and to hear him talk of roast-meat was as appetizing as a pickle or an oyster." Food is everything to this old sinecure. He possesses "no higher attributes" and devotes "all his energies and ingenuities to subserve the delight and profit of his maw." Worse, all else disappears. "A tenderloin of beef, a hind-quarter of veal, a spare-rib of pork, a particular chicken, or a remarkably praiseworthy turkey, which had perhaps adorned his board in the days of the elder

Adams, would be remembered; while all the subsequent experience of our race, and all the events that brightened or darkened his individual career, had gone over him with as little permanent effect as the passing breeze. The chief tragic event of the old man's life, so far as I could judge, was his mishap with a certain goose, which lived and died some

twenty or forty years ago; a goose of most promising figure, but which, at table, proved so inveterately tough that the carving-knife would make no impression on its carcass; and it could only be divided with an axe and handsaw."

That preoccupation with the maw is an image worse than that of Gluttony in *The Faerie Queene.*

A *weltanschauung* that cannot lead far.

But in our time we have one even more interesting: preoccupation with the navel. One's own.

We have eaten and rushed our merry lives into obesity and hypertension and now have the most marvelous concern with "superhealth" and "self-help." Yes, at this enlightened moment in the history of the human race, the middle-aged frump is not without aids. In the nick of time, movements, clinics, have sprung up and books have been written.

In prose less pedestrian but often more garish than that used for diets, the modern man in crisis has the self-help book. He can improve himself. He can know in a week, for $4.95, what the poor man of the Renaissance spent a lifetime learning; he can secure, not *good* health but "super" health.

The modern man can discover hidden inner energy. He can "get in touch with his feelings." There is immediate hope for his arthritis. He can quit smoking, without fail, in ten days. He can become his own best friend. He can learn body awareness, body language, body sensitivity. The orient provides its riches through acupuncture and shiatzu and meditation. Never have there been so many ways to cure hypoglycemia. Best, our modern man can become an artist in one month or a writer after one course—without tears, without pain.

We do not see much sense in pain today.

And sex? Don't ask. One would think, with all the manuals and tests and clinics and demonstrations and revelations that the human race had only recently discovered a few ways to satisfy the itch, that it could not learn "the new tenderness" without specific instruction.

Yes, we have unheard-of personal possibilities. You can be your own lawyer. You can find instant success and power. You can discover your erroneous zones. You can achieve instant (and multiple) gratification, instant enlightenment, instant wisdom, instant metamorphosis, instant health.

The nutritionist has ascended to the importance of the family physician, the family priest. If you run a mile a day, do fifteen minutes of the proper exercises, contemplate your navel, you are morally and spiritually and intellectually superior to him who merely slouches through his vale of tears.

Now "total health" can be yours. For $1,000 a week you can attend a "human-improvement center," a "fat farm." You can acquire, instantly, a new mind for that weary old one—and a new body. Surely the second coming is finally at hand.

Or are we merely buying new neuroses for old? Is it merely Emerson gone berserk? Is the "chief tragic event" of our lives becoming our astounding self-absorption—our inability to see a world out there that must be earned and learned with all the slowness and care that it takes for the best corn to ripen?

I don't know. Doesn't Yeats say that the soul *can* recover "radical innocence?" And that it can learn that

> ". . . it is self-delighting,
> Self-appeasing, self-affrighting,
> And its own sweet will is Heaven's will."

I suppose that's so. But Yeats also speaks about the "fascination of what's difficult" and about "The beating down of the wise/And great Art beaten down." A person can transform himself; the outer does affect the inner. But if it's all to mean much more than minor-league hedonism and solipsism, we'll have to remember that there is something called Art and that it is never easy, and that there is something called character, which you can't buy at discount or build in an hour.

JUNE 20

And so, at 165 pounds I have come to the end of this thing, the word and the flesh of it. Along the way I have discovered that I am not Peter Pan and that I cannot return to splendor at the courts or glory on the . . . well, glory anywhere. Sometimes I wish that I were young again, and could go for a double strawberry banana split, with three scoops of ice cream, whipped cream, nuts . . . but there are compensations. I look better and feel younger. I know

now that I do not have to devour the world. I have always been devoted to conservation of the physical world; now I'm also devoted to the conservation of me. But to be self-conserving and self-improving does not mean I have to become a nincompoop.

Now that my tendon is healed, I walk with a bounce again; I have more energy; my new clothes are the size I wore twenty years ago. I am thinking of returning one last time to the basketball courts. Mari is mad for my body. Sometimes.

Only this afternoon she came to me with a problem. With all the talk about food, she had gained three pounds. Old, slim Mari! And, without telling me, she has been trying to diet. "It's damned hard, you know," she said.

"It's nothing," I said, "Eat less. Exercise a little more. Go fishing now and then."

"I don't fish."

"Do those activities you truly like to do rather than hoping to beat the boredom of routine exercise. Fish. You really ought to get out trout fishing."

"I loathe fishing."

"Eat not as much as you can but as little as you need. All the diet books in the world cannot tell you one syllable more than this."

"Nick?"

"Resist the strudel. Once you've eaten it, what have you got? A moment's pleasure, hours of regret."

"I really did not ask for a lecture."

"Eat not to dullness, saith that wise old owl, Ben Franklin; eat particularly at some remove from starch and fat and sugar."

"Nick!"

"This leaves a lot to munch. Eat apples, especially at odd hours, but not oranges, which have too much natural sugar. Eat cantaloupes instead of honeydew for the same reason. Eat Swiss peasant bread and pita bread, which are delicious and nonfattening; farmer's cheese, an acquired taste, is excellent. But remember your Aunt Minnie's advice: 'Everything you put in *shows!*'"

"Must we talk about food? Must we?"

"Failing to find the thin person in you at first, keep encouraged; missing him at one meal, try at another: he stands someplace—lithe and gorgeous—waiting for you."

"Nick?" she said quietly.

"All right. What?"

"Will you please please please please *please* not talk about food and dieting anymore? *Please!*"